D1724911

DREAM WORLD OF DOLLS

DREAM WORLD OF DOLLS

FROM THE COLLECTION OF THE MUSEUM
OF FOLKLORE ANTWERP

Patricia Vansummeren

with contributions from
Katharina Engels, Françoise Therry

Photographs Bart Huysmans

SNOECK-DUCAJU & ZOON / PANDORA / CITY OF ANTWERP

Frontispiece: Cat. 1 / *Baby doll:*
'Margriet'
Belgium, early 18th century,
unmarked, h 67.5 cm
Completely in wood. Head and
torso finely carved and painted, open mouth, painted eyes
and hair.
Body, upper arms and legs
roughly carved, dark stain,
hinged shoulders, elbows,
thighs and knees. Lower arms,
hands and feet very finely
worked and painted.
Clothing (not original): cotton
underclothes, long christening
gown in organdie and lace.
VM 92.63.50

Table of contents

Foreword

Since its re-opening in 1988-1990 the Museum of Folklore has held one or more exhibitions per year with folkloric customs and traditions as the central theme. In the current exhibition, under the title 'The dream world of dolls', it is not the world of adults but the world of children that stands central. Dolls and their accessories make us look back to our childhood years when toys played an important part in our lives, especially from a pedagogical standpoint. Reference to ones childhood years is an essential part of the life cycle, and a theme that is frequently seen in folklore. We also offer a sociological aspect, illustrated in the contrast between the simple and often self made dolls of the people and the luxurious toys of the middle classes.

The Museum of Folklore's collection of toy dolls contains more than 270 pieces, and originates mainly from the two previous exhibitions that took place in Antwerp in 1916 and 1934.
The 1934 exhibition was organized by the Municipality of Antwerp with the cooperation of the 'Museum of Folklore'. Now sixty years later, the Museum of Folklore is once again holding a large exhibition around the theme of Dolls, this time based on it's own collection that is also being shown to the public in its totality for the first time.

The exhibition is divided into two sections. The main section shows 128 of the most interesting and best preserved dolls, while the rest of the doll collection is exhibited in a reserve formation for study purposes.

I would like to thank the extended team of collaborators who were responsible for the composition of the exhibition and the catalogue. The research for this exhibition was undertaken by Patricia Vansummeren, assistant at the Museum of Folklore, who was also responsible for the selection of the exhibits.

The practical realisation of the exhibition was provided by Françoise Therry, textile conservator for the Historical Museums, who as well as the conservation and restoration work of the dolls was also responsible for the presentation, and Ann Op de Beeck, designer for the Historical Museums, who determined the total concept of the exhibition. She was assisted in this by the complete personnel of the Museum of Folklore. I would also like to thank Geertrui Pas, educational co-worker of the MUHKA for her advice on the educational aspects of this exhibition.

A special word of thanks must also go to the authors who contributed to the catalogue; Katharina Engels, owner of the 'Puppen und Spielzeugmuseum' in Rothenberg ob der Tauber, who gave us permission to use her text on the technical developments of the doll as well as Marc Wellens, scientific assistant at the Toy Museum in Mechelen, who was responsible for the Dutch reworking and translation of this text. Françoise Therry described the conservation and restoration of the dolls while Patricia Vansummeren discussed the origins of the Museum of Folklore's doll collection. She also provided the illuminating catalogue notations.

The technical realisation of the catalogue was carried out by Bart Huysmans, photographer for the Office of Cultural Promotion and International Cultural Relations who took the photographs. The catalogue was printed and published by Snoeck-Ducaju & Zoon, Gent.

Our thanks also go to the Archaeological Excavation Department of the Museums of History and Applied Art of Antwerp, who were willing to lend an object for the exhibition.

Finally I would like to thank the Director Dr. Francine de Nave, who together with Frank Herreman, assistant director and Mireille Holsbeke, scientific assistant, were responsible for the coordination of this exhibition.

H.B. COOLS
Mayor

Preface

The restructuring of the municipal museums in 1991, saw the Museum of Folklore become part of the Historical museums group. In order to strengthen and enlarge this museum group into a firm entity the Museums of Folklore and Ethnography were merged into a single unit, at the end of 1993. The visual realisation of this project will probably not be immediately obvious to visitors as both museums need renovations in order to provide direct access from one museum to the other. The symbiosis of the contents is however, already in preparation, permanent exhibitions based on special themes are being planned that will compliment and combine the collections of both museums.

'The Dream World of Dolls', is an example of this new internal cooperation. This exhibition came to fruition, with the help of the personnel of both institutions, even though the exhibition is based mainly on the Museum of Folklore's collection. This selection can be viewed from a regional as well as a European perspective, and not only brings the best collection pieces to the publics attention but also provides a taste of the very worthy legacy that has been inherited by the new and enlarged folkloric section as a result of the merging of the museums of folklore and ethnography. These collections have remained, until now, relatively unknown, despite their obvious social-historical and cultural anthropological importance. We hope, therefore, that this exhibition will encourage further research and that the catalogue that accompanies the exhibition will also provide an added impetus for further study.

This reference work was compiled by Patricia Vansummeren, with contributions from Katharina Engels and Françoise Therry and illustrated with some remarkable photographs by Mr. Bart Huysmans, of the municipal video centre, and gives a number of technical details on every doll in the exhibition. This work is printed and published by the firm Snoeck-Ducaju & Zoon, and is available in Dutch and English. An English version has been published to address a more international public. An exhibition is temporary, a publication permanent.

We would like to give a special thank you to Mr. Bartel Baccaert, director of the publishing firm Snoeck-Ducaju & Zoon for his enthusiastic participation with the realisation of this book. We are also convinced that this work will not only be appreciated by institutions but will also be of some help to the many private dolls collectors both nationally and internationally.

We view this exhibition as the first in a series of similar manifestations that will help to make the municipal folkloric collections, which houses about one hundred and eighty thousand pieces, more accessible to the general public. These very rich collections offer many possibilities for an exhibition cycle, that will allow the diverse aspects of the daily lives of the people of Antwerp, in their diverse social sections to be brought into the public.

DR. FRANCINE DE NAVE
Director

FRANK HERREMAN
Associate director

ILL. I / Mike Kelley, 'Dialogue
#7 (Ambiguity and Amor-
phousness)'
Courtesy Galerie Jablonka,
Cologne, Copyright Bernard
Schaub, Cologne

Introduction

... on the table, on which they were placed, there were several other playthings; but that which attracted the eye the most was a pretty castle made of cardboard. One could see through the windows into the rooms, and in front there were several small trees, standing round a piece of looking glass, which represented a lake, reflecting the wax swans that swam upon it. It was all pretty, but the prettiest of all was a little girl, who stood in the middle of the open door. She was also made of cardboard, but had a dress of the thinnest muslin, and a piece of blue ribbon for a scarf, fastened at the neck with a broach quite as big as her whole face. The little girl held both her arms stretched out, for she was a dancer, and one leg was raised so high that the Tin soldier could not discover it, so that he thought she, like himself, had only one leg. 'that would be just the wife for me,' he thought; 'but she is rather grand, living in a castle, whereas I have only a box, and that I have to share with twenty-four others. That is no place for her; but yet I must try to make acquaintance with her.'.....

The Brave Tin Soldier, Hans Andersen Fairy Tales

Who does not remember their childhood dreams when, just as in the story of the Tin Soldier, dolls and other toys in the room come to life at night.
The dream is a definite proof of the mimesis character of dolls, where identification is one of the central themes.
Dolls are the perfect model on which a child projects, its ideal world, dreams and yearnings, as well as its fears and negative impulses. Dolls are not only roll models for children, but also for mothers, and by association the whole community. While playing with dolls girls learn to prepare themselves for their future rolls as housewife, wife and mother.

The Museum of Folklore's collection of dolls mainly date from the second half of the 19th century and thus illustrate the typical 'Victorian' values so characteristic of the bourgeoisie of the time. The roll of loving wife, mother and industrious housewife is reproduced in all its aspects, up to and including lace edged underwear. It is striking that this imitative effect is not often found in the rag dolls of the working class. This is probably why rag dolls in all their awkwardness are seen as so much more sympathetic than their distant, unapproachable middle class sisters.

The fact that the doll can be considered not only as a positive roll model and symbol of domesticity, but can also represent the opposite image has not been lost on some contemporary artists. We are thinking here of the works of the American artist Mike Kelley, in which used and battered dolls and other cuddly toys are sitting or lying on blankets and look as if they have been found on the streets. In this way Mike Kelley offers a profound insight into the situation of the homeless people and ghetto residents of South central Los Angeles.

Mireille Holsbeke

12

The story of two exhibitions:
The history of the Museum of Folklore's doll collection

The growing interest in the collecting of dolls in the last few years can be seen in the success of regular doll auctions that show and sell old dolls as well as the newest doll creations in Belgium and other countries. The rise in the number of small doll ateliers that design and create their own dolls also seems to have been stimulated by this renewed interest. Yet the reproduction of old models still remains an interesting sphere for many people. New publications on the general history of dolls, those made by special ateliers or on doll collections held in public or private collections regularly appear and are probably a response to the increasing demand for specific and more detailed information about dolls. The collecting of dolls for their historical, antique or financial value is definitely a phenomenon of our times.

Pre 1900 the doll was viewed primarily as a toy, and in some cases as a decorative object. It was usually bought as a play friend for the children who generally had more than one doll. Broken, wooden or rag dolls were usually thrown away, but porcelain dolls, that were relatively expensive and only bought by well to do families, were generally kept. This was not however with the intention of starting a collection. Some dolls were obviously not meant to be played with but served as ornamental objects, such as those used by 19th century fashion houses to present their new collections.

The end of the 19th century saw the beginning of the first doll collections. These were composed of average dolls, manufactured in the period, and dressed in regional costumes. They served as souvenirs and bore witness to a yearning for the exotic and foreign cultures. Antique dolls, older than 75 years, were however seldom seen in these collections. This is understandable as very few 17th and 18th century dolls managed to defy the face of time. Those that did survive the hands of children, were scrupulously kept in family circles either as a curiosity or as a memento of a distant ancestor. These 19th century dolls, now coveted collectors items, did not at the time however belong to the realms of the antique object. They were still to recent to be seen as items worthy of collecting.

The beginning of the 20th century saw the registration of the first real doll collections, mainly in England, America and France. In 1905 the 'Société des

ILL. II / Inside view of the
Doll exhibition of 1916.

Amateurs de Jouets et Jeux Anciens' was formed in Paris, with the aim of bringing together toy collectors with an active interest in old dolls. Belgium also had a few active private collectors. The 'Association for the preservation of the Flemish popular traditions' under the chairmanship of M. Elskamp, had some national character dolls in its possession. These were later given to the Museum of Folklore.

After the First World War collecting became a more popular past-time, although little attention was paid to the quality of the doll or its maker. The financial value also appeared to be of little importance. The emphasis was still placed on souvenir dolls and those in historical clothing. The Musée des Arts Décoratifs in Paris had a fine collection of dolls in historical costumes and the German Emperor Wilhem also owned an exceptional collection of dolls in regional dress.

Since the 1960's and 70's there has been a steady rise in the number of doll collections as more and more people started to bring their collections in to the open. Through this we have seen a growth in the number of small private museums, that have often been well received by the public. Public collections have also played eagerly in on this toy and doll collection rage, so that in just about every country one finds some form of doll and toy museum. Some of the better known collections can be found in the Germanisches National Museum and the Toy Museum in Nürnberg, in the Musée National in Monaco where the important Gallia collection is housed and the Museum of Childhood in London. In Belgium the collection from the Toy Museum in Mechelen is the most well known.

The demand for dolls, especially from the 19th century has grown constantly. Even though doll making had already reached its high point and there was talk of the mass production of certain types during this period, it appears that, proportionally speaking, very few dolls were kept. Partly because of this scarcity the cost price of dolls has risen enormously, and we have seen an increase in the number of special doll auctions. The game of supply and demand has led to prices varying from a few hundred thousand to millions of Belgian franks for a special or extremely rare doll. The question that needs to be asked is whether the present situation can continue. There will probably be a time when this will come to an end and prices will evolve in more reasonable proportions.

THE HISTORY OF THE DOLL COLLECTION

Like many folkloric and historical museums, the Museum of Folklore in Antwerp has an extensive collection of dolls. These can be divided into five main groups:
1. theatre dolls: mainly originating from the diverse 'poesjes' theatres that were housed in Antwerp from the middle of the 19th century; 2. toy dolls; 3. tourist dolls; 4. a large collection of religious dolls from the closed convents and 5. dolls with diverse functions, such as window dolls and dolls used for magic purposes.

As the collection is so large – the theatre dolls alone number more than 250 pieces – we are only paying attention to the toy dolls. This collection has more than 270 dolls that can be dated from the early 18th century to 1970. The largest section is dated from between the late 19th century to 1934.

The origin of the Collection

The 'Association for the preservation of the Flemish popular traditions', under the leadership of Max Elskamp, donated its collection to the City of Antwerp in 1907 with the aim of starting a museum of folklore. The first catalogue of the museum, listed 2816 objects. Under the chapter heading 'Family and Family life: Childhood' in the second paragraph one finds the collection 'swaddling clothed dolls and dolls'. The numbers 606 to 629, 23 items, are taken up by diverse toy dolls. Only the folk dolls were shown, not one ornamental or porcelain doll was included in the collection. These porcelain dolls were, according to the norms of the folklore of the period, not examples of working class culture but belonged to the upper middle classes. The collection contained: 5 swaddling clothed dolls, 3 peg wooden dolls, 1 rag doll, 14 folk

dolls not specified but mainly in wood and one special doll: 'large sculptured wooden doll from the 18th century'. This refers to the doll 'Margriet' that will be discussed later.

Competition and Exhibition of 1916

In 1916, during the First World War, a number of prominent Ladies from Antwerp organised a doll competition and exhibition for the benefit of the National Committee 'Our Invalids House' (ILL. II and III).
To participate in the competition one could either buy a doll or borrow one from the committee, and then dress it following a specific theme. Groups and schools were also invited to take part. The result of this action was 235 single designs and 45 groups of 196 dolls. At the end of the exhibition and after the awarding of the prizes, the dolls were sold in aid of 'our invalid

ILL. III / Little Red Riding hood and the wolf, Doll exhibition of 1916.

ILL. IV / Diploma given to doll cat. 31, pg. 69 at the Doll exhibition of 1916.

house'. The funds raised were used to provide help and shelter for war invalids. After the exhibition a publication was produced with photographs of all the dolls, the honour committee and the organisers of the exhibition. The dolls were presented under certain themes, such as occupations, fairy tale figures, the Virgin of Antwerp, the four seasons and so forth. From this we can see that no attention was paid to the quality of the dolls or their makers. What was represented was more important than the doll itself. Prizes were awarded for the prettiest or the most exceptionally dressed doll.

The town council decided to support the action by buying the doll groups made by the schools for the then Museum of Folklore. Which dolls were bought is unknown as there is no mention of these dolls in the acquisition register of the period. The photographs taken at the exhibition are also unable to shed any light on this issue. One doll from the collection that was definitely in the competition for dressed dolls was donated to the museum at a later date by its owners (ILL. IV, CAT. 31, PG. 69). This doll, marked Jumeau Médaille d'Or Paris, and dressed in a light green gown with matching hat, received a diploma at the exhibition for her participation, with the theme: Tribute to the Queen of Flowers.

International exhibition of old and modern dolls 1934

A second important doll exhibition took place in Antwerp in 1934, to benefit of the fund for unemployed clerical workers, following an initiative from the town Mayor Camille Huysmans. A special committee composed of a large number of prominent people from Antwerp was set up to oversee the exhibition.

The exhibition was placed under the protection of Her

Majesty Queen Astrid, who donated a number of dolls especially for the exhibition. This was an international exhibition, that showed dolls from other countries and the word 'doll' was taken in its widest sense. Historical and folk dolls, but also theatre dolls, Opsinjoorke from Mechelen and even the Giants from Lier, Mechelen and Borgerhout were shown. Schools and groups were again invited to make group scenes, as in 1916.
The 1934 exhibition was a large scale event. It took place in the town 'feestzaal' on the Meir in Antwerp, – a building provided by the city council to hold gala events, exhibitions etc. – and was filled to the smallest corners. The architect Mr. J. Smolderen was responsible for the construction of the exhibition, that was divided into eight sections:

1. Historical, folkloric and ethnographic section from private collectors and diverse public collections in Belgium; 2. Foreign dolls: dolls on loan from other countries, mostly in folkloric or national costume; 3. Contemporary dolls: fashion dolls, ornamental dolls etc. These dolls were especially made for the exhibition; 4. Dolls in uniform; 5. Dolls houses; 6. Commercial section: where different stores were represented; 7. Advertising: groups, shops and companies that introduced themselves through the use of scenes created with dolls; 8. Schools and institutions: dolls on specific themes made by the pupils.

The former Museum of Folklore was represented at this exhibition by a large number of dolls and related figures that covered many diverse themes, such as the Antwerp procession and the 18th century garden figures. A catalogue with descriptions of the dolls was released after the exhibition. This exhibition, like that of 1916, paid little attention to toy dolls. The largest section of the exhibition was composed of ornamental and folkloric dolls. Toy dolls could only be found

amongst the exhibits from the Museum of Folklore, the ethnographic dolls from the Museum of Tervuren and the Royal Museum of Art and History in Brussels. The decision to show only folkloric dolls or dolls in historical clothing falls completely within the spirit of the time. Only truly historical dolls, pre 1800, were thought to be important. Dolls from the late 19th century did not yet belong to the realms of the antique. Contemporary dolls were only used to show historical clothing or to explain the evolution of clothing (PHOTO. CAT. 47, PG 19). A number of dolls were donated to the Museum of Folklore after the exhibition, amongst them were the magnificent groups of the Virgin of Antwerp with her two pages (CAT. 37, 38, PG. 32, 73), and diverse ornamental dolls in both 19th century costumes and clothing from the 1930's. The Swedish costume doll, donated by Queen Astrid (CAT. 50, PG. 85) and those in Italian Costume donated by the Queen of Italy (CAT. 51, PG. 86) also became part of the collection. These dolls could, to a great deal, be identified from photographs in the catalogue and the acquisition registers of the time. The exhibition was a great success and appears to have made an impression on the international public. In 1935 a similar exhibition was held in Paris and the Museum of Folklore was asked to lend it 16 dolls. A number of dolls were also lent to Straatsburg for an international exhibition there.

The collection grew sporadically after the Second World War, with only a few dolls being donated to the museum. This explains why there are so few post war dolls in the collection.

THE COLLECTION

The collection policy of the Museum of Folklore has never allowed for the acquisition of old dolls or the formation of a specific collection. It is for this reason that dolls have never been bought. The emphasis of the collection was placed on folk dolls that were usually hand made or that could be bought very cheaply. More luxurious dolls were kept only if they had been donated. The present policy does not allow for the building of a complete collection either. It is felt that this could create competition and conflict with specialised museums, such as the Toy Museum in Mechelen, which is definitely not the intention.

The fact that there has never been a specific buying policy, has definitely left its mark on the doll collection. Some types are very well represented while others are completely absent.

Diversity

The Museum of Folklore's collection is exceedingly diverse in nature and dates from the beginning of the 18th century to around 1970. All types are represented: Ornamental dolls, folk dolls, tourist and real toy dolls. The dolls are made from a wide range of materials including; wood, cloth, porcelain, wax, composition, wax-over-composition, papier-maché etc.

The collection, naturally, has a large number of folk dolls made from very simple materials such as straw, hemp, clay, wood and cloth. These dolls were mostly made from scraps, such as the typical rag dolls or the dolls made in clay from the brick works and were mainly found among the poorest sections of the community (CAT. 103, 104, PG. 133).

Simple dolls like the peg wooden dolls and the swaddling clothed dolls were exported in large numbers from the Grödnertal, and could be bought very cheaply at local markets. The dolls clothes had to be made by the buyer. Similar dolls found in this country were called prison dolls as according to legend they made by prisoners.

In stark contrast to these simple toy dolls stand the luxury dolls made between the late 19th and early 20th century by famous doll makers such as J. Steiner, E. Jumeau, Bru and Kestner. Our collection holds a number of fine examples of these dolls.

Our French section, although not large, does hold some special dolls. The house of Jumeau is well represented with 6 dolls varying in size from 28 to 60 cm. One doll with luxurious curly hair, marked Déposé E 25 (J) (on the head) and Jumeau Médaille d'Or Paris (on the body) has a beautiful leather chest with mirror, in which her clothes and other accessories are kept (CAT. 25, PG. 63). One remarkable doll is marked 'Bte S.G.D.G.' (on the head) and 'Le petit Parisien Bébé J. Steiner Marque Déposée Médaille d'Or 1889, Paris' (on the loins). Her exceptional height, 96 cm, and special clothing really do give her the appearance of a child. The beautiful blue eyes give the doll an

CAT. 47 / ORNAMENTAL DOLL
circa 1934
Unmarked, h 43 cm
Head in pressed cloth,
painted eyes and mouth,
black wig.
Body and limbs in cloth and
stoneware.
Clothing: red velvet coat and
skirt edged with leather,
matching hat and handbag;
painted shoes.
VM 10.133

19

exceptional character and can be moved with a handel behind the ear (ILL.V, CAT.27, PG.65)

Among the unmarked dolls one finds a few with French origins. A walking doll, wound up with a key, can probably be accredited to J. Steiner (CAT.92, PG.124), the specific facial features an open mouth and fine sharp teeth lead one to assume this. Two musical automatons can definitely be accredited to Vichy. Both dolls, a boy and girl are sitting on a bench (CAT.79, 80, PG.111, 112). The girl has an apple in her hand; the boy is wearing an asses hat. The original clothing is however missing. There are also some ornamental dolls of French origin. Two of these are fashion dolls, unmarked, but with a strong likeness to the so called 'Parisiennes' (CAT.4, 5, PG.43, 44). There are also two very nice decorative dolls that cover bonbon boxes (CAT.84, 85, PG.116, 35) These boxes carry the name of J. Boissier confiseur in Paris.

The German dolls are well represented. Famous names such as Armand-Marseille, Heubach-Koppelsdorf, Kämmer & Reinhardt and Simon & Halbig are regularly seen. Most of these dolls are fairly common types, such as mould number 390 from Armand-Marseille. There are also a few typical character dolls, e.g a boy in a sailor suit with a very stubborn expression (CAT.14, PG.52), and the small baby-dolls dressed in christening gowns or baby clothes (CAT.11, PG.49). Unfortunately the very well known dolls from Käthe Kruse are not in the collection, but we have two Steiff dolls (CAT.18, 19, PG.56, 57).

Belgian dolls are clearly under represented. There are only two dolls from the Unica firm, one of which is a recent example and dates from around 1970 (CAT.102, PG.132). We also have two dolls from the Wiltry firm in Grimbergen, one of these is a grenadier and the other represents the Antwerps Mayor Van Cauwe-

laert. These dolls were especially made for the 1934 exhibition.

The collection is dominated by a large number of unmarked dolls whose heads are made from pressed cloth. They are mainly fashion dolls with a few character dolls that were especially made for the 1934 exhibition. The fashion dolls show the evolution of clothing in the 19th century and offer a view of contemporary fashions. The character dolls are mainly farmers wives with very well modelled heads.

A few specific dolls, some of which have special functions deserve further mention. Firstly, a splendid King from a Neapolitan Christmas crib, dated to around the middle of the 18th century (CAT.88, PG.120).

ILL. V / GIRLS DOLL
France, 1889 - 1892
Marked on the head: J. Steiner Bte
S.G.D.G., on the loins: Le Petit
Parisien Bébé. J.Steiner Marque
Déposée Médaille d'or 1889
Paris; h 96 cm
VM 92.63.51. Detail of the
mark. (cat. 27, pg. 65)

This doll is part of a complete set of 59 figures attributed to the Bernini atelier. The figures were carved in wood by a very skilled craftsman.

Apart from the two Vichy automatons that have already been mentioned we also have a marot of unknown origin (CAT. 81, PG. 113) and a musician with cymbals that possibly dates from the late 18th to early 19th century (CAT. 78, PG. 110). The cymbals can be brought together using a handel attached to his arm. And finally our attention must pass to the oldest doll in the collection, that dates from the beginning of the 18th century (PHOTO. CAT. 1, PG. 2). This wooden doll is composed of a rudimentarily manufactured body with a well sculptured head, a lot of attention has also been payed to the hands and feet. There is a bizarre story attached to this doll, that we are repeating here as it was reported in the 1934 catalogue. 'The doll Margriet. Doctor Pierre Hoylaerts born in Betecom on the 6th of October 1686 and died in Antwerp on the 7th of February 1767, had an older sister who after becoming a widow lost her only child, a two year old daughter. The poor mother became crazy with grief. To try and lessen her pain a local artist was asked to make a wooden doll for her. The poor mother, in the belief that her child was still alive, gave this doll her unbounded love, surrounded her with tender care, dressed and undressed her continuously, and rocked her constantly in her arms'. The doll was donated to the Museum of folklore in 1907.

Just because of the fact that there has never been a specific acquisition policy, the Museum of Folklore's doll collection offers a good view of the way in which public collections grow. This is in stark contrast to private collections and specialized doll museums. Through its heterogeneous character it illustrates the tastes of the general public and the evolution of the form of the doll since the 18th century. The presence of several special and rare dolls make an interesting and uplifting collection that still has the ability to surprise.

Patricia Vansummeren

21

The technical evolution of the doll

The history of the doll has been widely written about in many diverse publications. Her development can also be seen in the wide use of the different materials that were popular during the periods that the dolls were manufactured.

The function of dolls was determined to a large degree by the materials used, children's toys were usually made from the most simple materials, such as wood and cloth while more luxurious dolls were made in bisque or porcelain. As the issue of the durability of dolls became more important, a search began for new, mostly industrially made, materials that could better withstand the rough treatment. One of these, celluloid was said to be 'unbreakable' by its makers. This was later mainly replaced by plastic and later vinyl for the production of dolls.

WOODEN DOLLS

Wooden dolls have been in use since antiquity and were mostly made from soft woods. It was not until the middle ages that the figures began to have shapes that could be compared with the dolls we know now. Wooden dolls were mainly used as offers (ex voto) in religious ceremonies, they later became a form of entertainment for the court household. Artists began to use peg wooden dolls as models around the beginning of the 17th century. Toy dolls were also made in these periods, but very few were kept.

In England 'Queen Anne Dolls' became popular from the beginning of the 1700's. These dolls had faces that were carved out of the wood, and painted eye brows, cheeks and mouth. Black glass eyes without pupils were sometimes used instead of paint. The bodies were simple and the limbs became jointed. Wooden dolls, 'Docken' from Sonneberg were made on a lathe, they had painted facial features and most of them wore hats. The arms were glued on and could only be moved on dolls with special pull mechanisms. Dolls from the Grodnertal were also turned, their noses being added later. The facial features were, like most wooden dolls painted, the limbs, joints and body

CAT. 110 / RAG DOLL
early 20th century
Unmarked, h 42 cm
Completely in cloth. Head with embroidered nose and mouth, eyes made from two pins, shawl round head. Body wound in red shawl, no arms or legs. *Clothing:* checked woollen skirt and Vichy apron.
VM 4657

were kept together by wooden pins and were completely moveable. The first report of these dolls dates back to approximately 1735.

Wooden dolls and dolls heads from the second half of the 19th century are mostly covered with a thick layer of paint. Some dolls were first covered in a layer of flesh coloured paint, then dipped in wax and finished with a layer of varnish. Production centres for these still primitive wooden dolls could be found in Berchtesgaden, Gröden and Sonneberg. In Sonneberg the turned round faces of the wooden dolls were first covered with a layer of bread dough then finished with plastic.

Peg wooden dolls from Gröden and Sonneberg were sought after articles in England at the beginning of the 1800. Queen Victoria is said to have dressed her wooden dolls in designs from the court. The dolls were from the Grödner valley and their style remained the same until the 1920's (PHOTO. CAT. 114, PG. 24).

WAX

Wax has been used since antiquity to make many different objects. In the late middle ages artists used this material to create figures and scenes. Wax is produced by bees but can also be found in plants. Heating liquifies the wax, thus making it easier to add chemical substances and/or paint to it. The production of small human figures in wax stems from the time when wax sculptures were going through a growth period, the late 18th – early 19th century. Exceptional pieces from this period include the Christmas Cribs, that show whole scenes created in wax. Wax heads, that were attached to small wooden lay figures (5 to 10 cm high), also bear witness to the folk artistry of the 18th and 19th centuries.

Inspired by these wax products and the later ateliers for wax figures, the use of wax was finally adapted to the manufacture of dolls heads. In the 1780's the Pierotti Family of London made startlingly accurate copies of children in wax. Pierotti and Montanari exhibited their figures and dolls at the 1851 World exhibition in London. In 1886 Heinrich Stier discovered a method

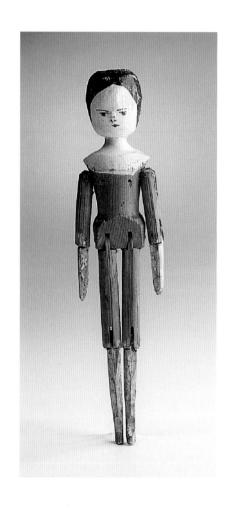

CAT. 114 / PEG WOODEN DOLL

Germany, 20th century
Unmarked: Grödnertal, h 32 cm.
Completely in wood, with movable limbs, head with painted eyes, mouth and hair.
VM 5325

of making wax heads in a casting mould. Wax dolls were on the market until the beginning of this century. Montanari – dolls, also copied in Sonneberg, had soft and round outer forms, while the Pierotti – dolls were more life like in shape and form. German wax dolls are easily recognised by the typical expression of the Sonnebergse 'ladies'. These dolls have the outward appearance of a lady and have in most cases blue eyes.

PAPIER MACHÉ – COMPOSITION

Papier-maché has been in use as a material since the 18th century. It is a very pliable substance made from cellulose or old kneaded paper and can be mixed with clay, chalk, colours, plaster and glue. Papier-maché can be pressed into a sulphur mould by hand, but can also be completely hand modelled.

The model makers Gottfried and Friedrich Müller from Sonneberg received permission in 1805 to use papier-maché in the manufacture of toys. The pieces were initially hand made, but inspired by the manufacture of tin toys, Müller developed sulphur moulds in which papier-maché could be pressed. These were the first papier-maché heads on the market. In 1822 Kestner received permission to work with papier-maché in Waltershausen.

Papier-maché dolls heads were covered with a layer of wax from 1852 onwards. These dolls were called 'Dopelingen' and became 'bestsellers' in Thüringen following the success of the World Exposition in London. On the 29th of April 1857 Motschmann took out a patent on a papier-maché doll. This doll would be known in the history of dolls as the 'Motschmann type', and was copied by many doll makers. Ludwig Greiner emigrated to Philadelphia in 1858 and took out a patent on a papier-maché dolls head known as the 'pumpkin heads'. These dolls had modelled hair styles, cheap bodies and wooden arms and legs. They were colourfully painted (usually with blue boots), and were sold en masse (mostly at fairs) (PHOTO. CAT. 127, PG. 26).

Papier-maché, mixed with other materials is often called 'composition'. This term is mainly used by collectors. Composition is usually made of different ingredients, with woodpulp mixed with glue as the main ingredient. Every doll maker however has his own secret recepie for this composition.

PORCELAIN

In the production of porcelain dolls heads one differentiates between, glazed porcelain, parian porcelain and bisque porcelain (PHOTO. CAT. 22, PG. 30).

In 1708 J.F. Böttger became the first person to produce porcelain. It is made from kaolin (also called porcelain earth), feldspar and quartz. The different components are finely ground and poured into a mould then painted, glazed and baked. Porcelain was first used to make dolls heads around 1840.

Schlaggenwald exhibited the first porcelain dolls heads in Vienna in 1845. Glazed porcelain dolls heads first have their facial features modelled and the eye brows, eyes and mouth painted. The hair was also modelled beforehand and painted either blond or black. Heads with torsos were placed on bodies made from cloth or leather. The arms and legs were also in

pg. 26:
Cat. 127 / GIRLS DOLL
pumpkin head, 19th century
unmarked, h 70 cm.
Head with torso in wax over composition, moveable glass eyes, closed mouth, painted hair.
Body and limbs in cloth and wood; feet and boots in painted wood.
Clothing: cotton underclothes, striped dress (black-red) with black apron made from satin and velvet.
VM 92.63.3

pg. 27:
Cat. 128 / DOLL
early 20th century
Unmarked, h 72 cm
Head and torso in celluloid, sleeping eyes, open mouth, painted eye brows and eye lashes, flax wig.
Body and upper legs in leather, cloth upper arms, stoneware lower arms, celluloid lower legs and feet.
Clothing: long cotton shirt, cotton dress, velvet coat and matching bonnet with a rosette in the Belgian colours.
VM 60.132.1

porcelain and had painted shoes or button boots. This type of doll known as the 'Biedermeier doll' was manufactured for many years without any substantial changes. The glazed heads were usually modeled on famous people such as Queen Victoria, Jenny Lind and Fanny Elssner. In the 1860's the first bath dolls 'Frozen Charlotte' appeared on the market. These dolls were completely made from porcelain and were produced until the 1930's.

PARIAN PORCELAIN

Parian porcelain was discovered in England. It is composed of silica, clay, chalk, sodium and magnesium. Dolls heads made from this type of porcelain are white and only the facial features such as the eyes, mouth and cheeks were painted. The majority of these dolls had beautifully modelled hair styles, and the best examples had glass eyes.

The dolls bodies were usually made from cloth or leather, the arms and legs from porcelain or papier – maché. Here too we see the use of famous people as a 'sales ploy', for example Empress Eugenie (Napoleon the IIIrd's wife) and Empress Augusta-Victoria (wife of Wilhelm IInd). The hair styles were accessorised with diadem, flowers, hairnets and jewellery. The heads with torso in parian often used the bust as the upper part of the clothing, or modelled it as a collar. Small labels, or titles and names were also attached. The painting was very finely finished.

BISQUE PORCELAIN

This is composed of the same materials as normal porcelain kaolin, feldspar and quartz, but is baked twice and in contrast to porcelain, left unglazed.

CAT. 121 / DOLLS HEAD
Germany, early 20th century
Marked: 370 AM 12/0 Armand
Marseille Made in Germany,
h 11 cm
Porcelain head with torso,
blue sleeping eyes, open
mouth with teeth, painted
eye brows, blond woollen
wig; pointed felt cap with
two pompons.
VM 92.63.17

The kaolin found in the ground in Thüringen was especially suitable for the manufacturing of bisque porcelain. This material had been in use since the 18th century and had been mainly employed in the making of statuettes and figures. It was not however a popular material until new techniques allowed it to be applied to the making of dolls. Bisque porcelain underwent a period of new growth as dolls heads made in this material have a skin that appears to be almost real (PHOTO. CAT. 121, PG.28).

French dolls stand out because of their beautiful expressions and especially nice eyes. French fashion dolls were made from a very clear and fine quality bisque. It is not known whether bisque heads were first manufactured in France or Thüringen. Hurét received a patent on a 'shoulder head with weight' (swivel neck), in Paris in 1860, this patent was later also used by Jumeau. The bodies of Huréts fashion dolls were made in wood and completely moveable. In 1870 Emile Jumeau's new factory in Montreuil began to make its own bisque porcelain dolls heads.

By 1880 Thüringen had completely changed over to the production of bisque porcelain and the growth period of the toy doll had begun. Heads with torsos – the head often slightly bent – were mounted on leather bodies. Heads with joints were placed on wooden bodies. There were also many new types of dolls brought onto the market. Swimming dolls with moveable arms and legs, talking dolls and walking dolls all appeared in the shops during this period. By 1900 there were more than 100 porcelain factories in Thüringen. Character dolls appeared from 1905 and were a definite change from the stereotypical faces of the earlier porcelain dolls. Kämmer & Reinhardt's character dolls with serial numbers from 100 to 128, were put on the market at this time. Around 1910 the

first baby dolls with bent limbs were developed. In 1912 standing babies made in the image of 1 to 2 year old children caused a sensation at the toy market in Leipzig. Although the First World War had limited the markets and export areas, by 1919 German dolls were again in great demand overseas, especially in America.

Almost all dolls with bisque heads have a makers mark on the back of the head or on the underside of the torso. The numbers usually refer to the patent or other form of legal copyright and the letters show the initials of the maker.

CLOTH

Through the centuries cloth dolls have been made for home use (PHOTO. CAT. 110, PG.22). The first examples to be made in small ateliers were exhibited by Montanari at the 1851 world exhibition in London. Linen, felt and muslin were used. Cloth dolls made from printed rag material that one could cut out and finish came from America, and usually had names such as 'Henriette' of 'rag doll'.

Margarete Steiff started a cloth doll factory in 1878, her first felt dolls appeared in 1898.

In 1919 an Italian named Lenci brought felt artists dolls onto the market. The body, face and clothing were all made from felt, they had mohair wigs and very colourful clothing. The faces had either a very cheeky or a stubborn expression. Some of the dolls had large moveable glass eyes (called saucer eyes). Lenci dolls are still produced in Italy as they were in 1919.

In 1910 Käthe Kruse brought her dolls onto the market. She wanted to produce an unbreakable, durable doll that was light weight and moved like a baby.

The hair and face were painted. In 1922 the 'Schlenkerchen' (little rascal) and the 'Träumerchen' (the dreamer) models were released. The 'German child', a true copy of Friedbald, Käthe Kruse's four year old son, was introduced in 1929 with a real hair wig. The faces of Käthe Kruse dolls were unique in that instead of the typical painted facial features, she covered the face with a layer of water resistant muslin into which she pressed different oil colours to represent the eyes, cheeks, mouth etc.

Käthe Kruse dolls were very well finished, lovingly dressed and usually had very extensive wardrobes. There are still six different Käthe Kruse dolls produced, three of which are old models. Here too there is a great deal of diversity in the dolls clothing, that is finely worked to the last detail. Unfortunately we do not have any examples of her work in the collection.

CAT. 22 / GIRLS DOLL

France, late 19th century
Marked: on head Dep. 10,
on body Jumeau Médaille d'Or
Paris, h 51 cm
Porcelain head, glass eyes, closed mouth, painted eye brows and eye lashes, pierced ears, real hair wig with plait.
Body and limbs in composition, ball and socket joints.
Clothing: cotton underclothing, striped dress, white cotton apron.
VM 58.53.6

CELLULOID

Celluloid was discovered in 1869 by the Hyat brothers (USA). This discovery led to the first attempts to manufacture dolls in celluloid. The breakthrough of celluloid was not a simple matter however due to its inflammability. The first celluloid dolls did not appear on the market until 1894. This was due to the long periods of experimental work undertaken at the Rheinischen Gummi and celluloid factory in Mannheim (Schildkröt), on, amongst other things, the problems associated with the inflammability of celluloid. The dolls were made from two pre moulded halves glued together, with moveable limbs and painted facial features (PHOTO. CAT. 128, PG. 27).

The development of celluloid dolls runs parallel with that of the rest of the doll industry. In 1910 celluloid character babies were put on the market. Schildkröt produced 'cellowax heads' and 'mibluheads' for the Thüringen doll industry. The so called 'miblu heads' manufactured by Kämmer & Reinhardt gave the dolls a more life like appearance; like milk and blood hence the acronym Miblu-milk and blood in german. Celluloid is a very light and thin but very stable material. Through the centuries different materials have been used to manufacture dolls; wood, textiles, wax, papier-maché, porcelain, vinyl etc. These developments show the evolution of dolls from those made by hand and in small ateliers to the industrially manufactured dolls. There is at the moment a tendency towards a re-establishing of the artisanal approach to the making of dolls in both textiles and porcelain. This movement runs parallel with the modern hyper sophisticated electronic doll industry.

Original German text by Katharina Engels
Dutch reworking: Marc Wellens

Dolls through the eye of a needle
The report of the conservation techniques

Just as everything in this world is perishable, so to is the collection of dolls from the Museum of Folklore which have not escaped the fate of aging, decaying, breaking and to a greater or lesser degree crumbling to dust. Around 70 dolls from the collection needed more than just a spring clean. Their restoration – or better said conservation was started from a different viewpoint than that which one would normally expect; in other words renewing the dolls, such as a new pair of eyes or a wig, repainting and retouching the facial features, repair of walking or other mechanisms, replacement or tightening of connecting elastic between both arms or legs etc. Such intervention did not occur, except for one or two exceptional circumstances. The main purpose of the treatment was to stop any further decay so that they could be left in a better condition for future generations. This mainly consisted of removing many layers of dust and dirt and the remains of vermin and mildew from the dolls, where possible they were cleaned, the clothes washed and damaged clothing consolidated. I will describe the different work methods depending on the materials used to make the dolls.

PORCELAIN – GLASS

A large number of the dolls have porcelain parts: head – arms – hands – legs – feet – torso; and glass eyes. In view of the relatively stable nature of these materials, they could be cleaned without any problems. The porcelain and glass was cleaned with a cotton bud soaked in a solution of demineralised water and a neutral detergent, then 'rinsed' a number of times to ensure that no residue from the detergent remained and dried with cotton wool. Extra attention was needed to ensure that there was no contact made with body parts in another material, especially the wigs and their excess glue residues, as they are water soluble. If the excess glue residues interfered with the aesthetic aspect of the doll and were not essential for the fixing of the wig, they were carefully scrapped away with a wooden spatula. By some types of porcelain where the

CAT. 37 / THE VIRGIN OF ANTWERP
Germany, early 20th century
Marked: Heubach-Koppelsdorf
312 Sur 6 Germany, h 74 cm
Porcelain head, glass eyes, open mouth with teeth, real eyelashes, wig with long blond plaits decorated with flowers.
VM 10.100

glaze was still slightly porous, attention had to be paid to ensure that no drip-lines were caused through the use of excess moisture. These streaks are difficult to remove and call for extra rubbing which, considering the porosity, is best avoided. The results of the cleaning were mostly extremely good (ILL. VI)

COMPOSITION

The majority of the treated dolls are made in this material: different body parts are modelled on a base of papier-maché on which layers of plaster, coloured plaster, a paint layer and finally varnish (not always) are placed. The quality of dolls created in this manner varies a great deal depending on the doll maker.
In spite of the layer of varnish, this material proved to be porous. This was caused by quality differences and aging of the varnish, deterioration and irregularly applied varnish layers. A lot of precautionary measures needed to be taken before I could clean this material. A soft brush together with a specially adapted vacuum cleaner, more of which later, was used to remove the surface dust and dirt, thus ensuring that the dust did not penetrate deeper into the material. Spots of ingrained dirt were removed with a wooden spatula, or if possible with a slightly moistened cottonbud (ILL. VII). We first ensured that the varnish layer was not water soluble, by testing it on a place that was not directly visible such as the sole of the foot or the back of the ear.

The results of the cleaning were variable, depending on the amount of dirt and whether or not it could be wet cleaned. This was done with a solution such as demineralised water, with or without a small amount of agepon (= a product that reduces the surface tension of the water) or simply with saliva. We did try to give two dolls a more thorough cleaning, with a doubtful result. Both of these dolls had lost some of their aesthetic value due to the deterioration of the material caused by normal use.

ILL. VI / Porcelain head from 'The virgin of Antwerp', partly cleaned. (cat. 37, pg. 32)

CAT. 85 / ORNAMENTAL DOLL BON-BON BOX

France, late 19th century
Doll unmarked. h 42 cm
Mark on box: Boissier Confiseur
7 B. des Capucines Paris
Head in porcelain with glass eyes, closed mouth, painted eye lashes and eye brows, ear rings, blond wig.
Body consists of a cardboard box, arms and legs in porcelain.
Clothing: cotton underclothes, silk dress, lace veil, satin shoes.
VM 60.9.254b

ILL. VII / Cleaning of doll in composition with a slightly dampened cotton bud, this process can only be used if the varnish layer is insoluble.

ILL. VIII / Using binoculars while cleaning a very brittle paint layer on a wooden dolls head.

WOOD

Wood is naturally a porous material and thus difficult to clean, even if it is painted. After careful dusting this material was tested to see if it could be wet-cleaned, where necessary. The paint layer on the face of the doll (CAT. 59, PG. 94) was badly cracked and was coming away from the wooden under layer. It was cleaned under binoculars so as to have a clear view of the work and to prevent material loss (ILL. VIII). This method was very intensive, and we therefore only aimed to make the eyes more expressive; they had become dull through being buried in dust. On the other hand there were no problems with the doll (CAT. 72, PG. 104). This paint layer was very stable and could be cleaned with cotton buds, moistened in a solution of demineralised water and agepon. The result is all the more stunning as she was exceptionally dirty.

LEATHER

A number of dolls have leather limbs and trunks in leather filled with sawdust. The leather was mainly white, of a very fine quality, and mostly in good condition. There were in some places a few loose seams, deterioration and loose rusty metal pins that stuck through the leather. Water or another kind of solvent could not be used: dust and dirt was brushed off with a soft paintbrush, stubborn spots with a slightly harder paintbrush while making sure that the leather pores were not damaged and that the dirt did not penetrate any deeper. This had varying results. Cotton wool was used to replace the lost sawdust, and the loose seems were re sewn with cotton thread making use of the old holes. The iron pins were carefully pushed back into place and the hole covered with a linen 'bandage'.

This was done to prevent the pins from moving again and to protect the doll's clothes.

WAX

Three of the treated dolls had heads or other body parts in either wax or wax-over-composition. Wax is a very delicate material: dust and dirt particles were stuck to the surface or had penetrated more deeply, ugly scratches disfigured the entire area. We did not expect any spectacular results here. A soft paintbrush was used to remove the surface dust and a slightly damp cotton wool ball was used in an attempt to give a more thorough cleaning: the rubbing remained visible and the colour came off of the painted parts (hair). It therefore remained by the one attempt.

TEXTILES

There were many diverse sorts of textiles that needed treatment: wool, linen, cotton, silk, synthetic materials and others. At the same time a distinction had to be made as to the function of the textile: whether it was clothing of whether it formed a part of the construction of the doll. Dolls made from textile materials such as felt, pressed cotton, painted and covered with silk or artificial silk, and rag dolls were vacuumed with the help of a specially adapted household vacuum cleaner: an extension piece was placed on the suction pipe, this consisted of a plastic tube that was able to resist the pressure and a glass pipette. This adaptation allowed us to accurately clean small areas without material loss and with a minimum of risk to the materials as a result of suction. The faces of the pressed cloth dolls had to be treated with the utmost care, as the paint layer from the facial features and the taut silk muslin covering

were very brittle.

Parts in felt, wool and to a lesser extent silk (such as silk wigs) often appeared to have been attacked by vermin. Although all the affected dolls had undergone a special gas treatment in a gass bubble, this was carried out by a specialised firm, and the vermin had been destroyed, the remains of the larva, cocoon and the eggs still had to be removed with a pair of tweezers and the dolls vacuum cleaned. An annual control of the dolls will be necessary in the future. An anti moth treatment could not be carried out, as the long term damage the product might cause to the dolls could not be foreseen.

THE CLOTHING: CLEANING AND CONSERVATION TECHNIQUES

If one wants to clean the clothes then it would seem, at first sight, obvious that one undresses the doll. This is however not always the case. Attention must be paid to a few points, such as:
– is it *necessary* to remove the clothes? e.g. very dirty or bad condition.
– *can* the clothing be taken apart without creating too many problems for the re assembling of the clothes. For textile conservation reasons one should not dismantle the clothing: if seams, stitches etc are cut and removed the original character of the treated object is lost to some degree. Although I support this standpoint, I do believe that there can be some exceptions to the rule. I would like to explain this with a few examples.

Ornamental dolls, folkloric dolls and some fashion dolls (used as models for fashion designers and their distributers) appear to have been clothed in such min-

37

ute detail that their dismantling would cause unforseen difficulties and problems at a later date. These dolls were however, due to their limited use, not too dirty so that careful and thorough vacuuming was enough to produce a satisfying result in all but two cases. The exceptions were two fashion dolls that had large areas of mildew. One of them (CAT. 5, PG. 44) was carefully undressed: the velvet jacket, belt and silk dress were washed in a bath of white spirit; the cotton underclothes were washed in water with a neutral detergent. With the other doll (CAT. 46, PG. 82) we first removed the cloak and then dismantled the dress: the stitches in the knot of the cloaks scarf and the drapery stitches of the dress were cut, after a sketch and notes had been made of the original mode of dress.
The argument in defence of this intervention was the presence of mildew, that posed a real danger of infecting the rest of the collection and the fact that some mildews are dangerous to humans. The dress and cloak were cleaned in a bath of white spirit. The clothes were not vacuumed beforehand to minimise the spread of the spores and to lower the risk of contamination. Both the treatments and the reassembling occurred without any problems.

One last example of dismantling is the bon bonnière (PHOTO. CAT. 85, PG. 35). The lace veil and the edging on the dress (synthetic? machine made lace) were in a pitiful state. The manipulation of the doll while cleaning and vacuuming all the parts would have resulted in such a loss of material and lace work that I decided to remove the veil, having first made a drawing of the way in which the material fell over the head and upper body. It proved possible to reconstruct the total length and breadth of the veil as it was mainly the tulle underground that had perished and thus the cohesion of the veil. All the fragments were placed on a glass plate in

the correct order. This worked because of a chalk drawing of the repetitive motif in the lace work. All the fragments were sprayed with a fine mist of demineralised water, the excess water was blotted with acid free blotting paper. This treatment was repeated twice because of the amount of dirt. At the same time the veil was laid straight and in shape, then dried in the open air. The veil was then fixed to a piece of silk muslin using running stitches that followed the contours of the motif, using special two thread silk (ILL. IX).

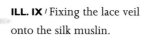

ILL. IX / Fixing the lace veil onto the silk muslin.

The excess muslin was carefully cut along the edges of the veil. The lace edging of the dress was reconstructed using the same method, and reattached to the dress. The silk dress itself was very dusty which gave it a grey drab appearance. In spite of the fine look of the drapery, the stitching was crude. I also decided to remove the dress to wash it in water with a neutral detergent then to dry it in form. The treatment of this doll was very radical and labour intensive, but the result was definitely worth it.

The situation was different with the toy dolls: the clothing could be easily put on and taken off (part of the fun of playing with dolls is dressing and undressing them). It is interesting to note the quality of the underclothes: vests – underpants – petticoats in fine cotton – or linen batiste with bobbin lace edges – english lace, open work – white embroidery, bows and ribbons, and embroidered initials. This contrasts with the outer clothes, that were often made of recycled materials or had a more used and old aspect to them, they are the top layer and are thus the most vulnerable part of the clothing.

The majority of these pieces of clothing were first vacuumed then washed in water with a neutral detergent, rinsed, carefully blotted with sponge towels and then dried flat in the open air. Pieces of coloured clothing were first tested for colour fastness: a small piece of thread (2-3 mm) of each colour was taken from a non visible place (eg. inside seams as one often finds loose threads on the inside of the clothing). The sample was heated in a test tube with a solution of neutral detergent until it reached boiling point, then cooled and the solution controlled for colouration. If the colour had run, then the item was not washed in water and was usually left in its original condition. Cleaning with a solvent such as white spirit, could be

considered, but was not used here, except in the case of the clothing that was affected with mildew as mentioned above.

THE TREATMENT OF WIGS IN HUMAN HAIR, SILK, SYNTHETIC SILK, WOOL AND OTHER MATERIALS

The greatest difficulty here is to prevent too great a loss of material. The matted aspect of the wigs is mainly caused by the hair and hair locks coming away from the base. We chose to use a minimum of intervention to achieve a reasonable result: careful yet through vacuuming, and the use of a not too hard brush or paint brush to achieve the desired hairstyle.

CONCLUSION

The dictionary defines crawling through the eye of a needle as: escaping from a great danger. It was not my intention to give the title of my report such a radical meaning.

Rather: the eye of the needle: you have to be able to *see* well to thread a needle: to see, to observe, to take notes are the first important steps in any conservation treatment. Then: what can one undertake in order to; run the minimum risks to the object while attempting to limit the damage and halt the aging process, and to carry out these treatments to the best of our ability without loosing sight of the effect this will have now and in the future.

Françoise Therry

39

The collection of the museum of folklore.

I. Moi je suis née dans une rose.

II. Poupée fut trouvée dans un sabot de Noël.

IV. Fais dodo, ma mignonne.

V. Oh! la méchante

Overview: origin and history

VI. Ne pleure plus, ma chérie.

VII. Embrasse moi, poupée.

VIII. Envoie un baiser.

IX. En toilette pour la prome

2

3

2 / BUST

early 19th century
Unmarked, H 16 cm
Female bust in papier-maché,
with closed mouth, glass
eyes, painted eye brows and
modelled hair style.
VM 5561

3 / BUST

early 19th century
Unmarked, H 18 cm
Female bust in porcelain,
with closed mouth, painted
eyes, eye brows and cheeks.
Real hair wig held together
in a hairnet, velvet ribbon
with bow.
VM 5459

**4 / ORNAMENTAL –
FASHION DOLL**

France (?), late 19th century
Unmarked, H 46 cm
Porcelain head with glass
eyes, closed mouth, painted
eye brows and eye lashes,
earrings, real hair wig.
Body and limbs in
leather.

Clothing: cotton underclothes,
coat and skirt in striped
material with train, jacket
with rose shaped buttons.
VM 58.53.8

44

8

pg. 44:

5 / ORNAMENTAL – FASHION DOLL

France (?), late 19th century
Unmarked, H 44 cm.
Porcelain head with glass eyes, closed mouth, painted eye brows and eye lashes, wig missing.
Body and limbs in leather.
Clothing: cotton and satin underclothes, brown velvet dress decorated with beads, leather boots.
VM 9762

pg. 45:

6 / GIRLS DOLL

pre 1850
Unmarked, H 48 cm.
Head with torso in wax over composition, glass eyes that shut via a mechanism in the back, closed mouth.
Body in cloth and composition, limbs in wood and composition.
Clothing: cotton underclothes, striped silk dress, imitation leather shoes.
VM 10.108

7 / PEG WOODEN DOLL

Germany, 19th century
Unmarked: Grödnertal,
H 26.5 cm.
Completely in wood, with movable limbs, head with painted eyes, mouth and hair.
VM 4487

7

marked German dolls

8 / DOLLS, GERMANY

circa 1912
Marked: Heubach-Koppelsdorff
250 19/0 Germany H 16 cm.
Porcelain head with painted eyes, mouth and eyebrows, mohair wig.
Body and limbs in composition.
Clothing: Hungarian Costume, cotton underclothes, wide cotton skirt, blouse and apron in organdie, shoulder bands decorated with interlace and beads, head scarf.
VM 5515-5516.

9 / GIRLS DOLL 'REINE DE SABA'

Germany, early 20th century
Marked: Armand Marseille 390 A
4 M Made in Germany, H 47 cm
Porcelain head, sleeping eyes, open mouth with teeth, no wig.
Wooden body with joints.
Clothing: long damask gown, over gown in tulle with gold coloured buttons, with long train.
VM 10.109

10

12

12

pg. 48:

10 / BRIDE

Germany, after 1894
Marked 1894 Am 1 DEP Made
in Germany Armand Marseille,
H 38cm
Porcelain head, sleeping
eyes, open mouth with teeth,
painted eyebrows and eye-
lashes, woollen wig.
Body and limbs in wood.
Clothing: cotton under
clothes, silk brides dress with
a long wide train, lace veil,
brides bouquet, silk socks
and shoes.
VM 60.9.172

pg. 49:

11 / BABY DOLL

Germany, early 20th century
Marked: Armand Marseille A.M.
Germany 351 K, H 23 cm
Porcelain head, sleeping
eyes, open mouth with teeth,
painted hair.
Porcelain arms. Body com-
posed of a metal spring
covered with material.
Clothing: cotton underclothes,
christening gown with lace
and broderie, lace bonnet.
VM 89.75.9

12 / TWINS

Germany, post 1890
Marked: Armand Marseille 390
7/10 Made in Germany,
H 31 cm
Heads in porcelain, one with
brown and one with blue
sleeping eyes, open mouth
with teeth, painted eye
brows and eye lashes, blond
wigs.
Body, limbs and hands in
leather with moveable legs
and knees.
Clothing: cotton petticoat,
blue linen coat with lace on
the sleeves and hem.
VM 92.63.36, 92.63.37

13 / CHARACTER DOLL

early 20th century
Marked: Kämmer & Reinhardt
30, H 31 cm
Head in porcelain, painted
eyes, closed mouth.
Body and limbs in composition.
Clothing: cotton underclothes,
low waisted floral dress,
leather shoes.
VM 59.14.822

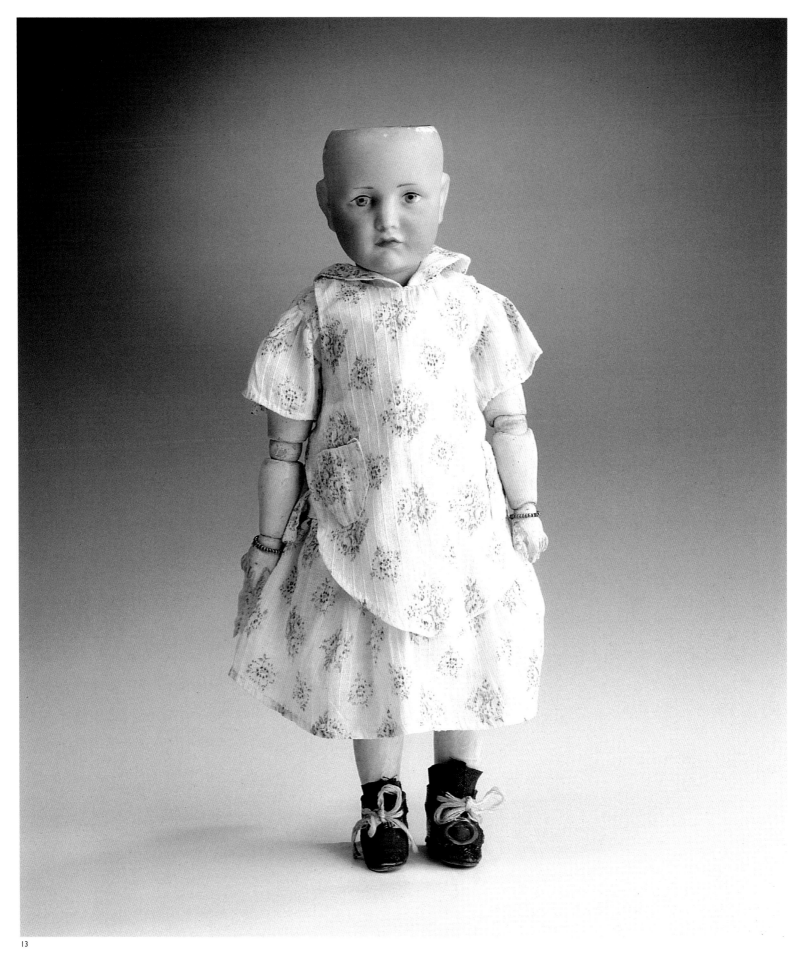

14

15

14 / CHARACTER DOLL

Germany, early 20th century
Marked: on head: 149 5°
on body: Kämmer & Reinhardt,
H 42 cm
Porcelain head, brown sleeping eyes, closed mouth,
painted eye brows and eye
lashes, real hair wig.
Body in composition; limbs
in composition and wood
Clothing: sailor suit with flannel under shirt, silk socks,
imitation leather shoes.
VM 59.14.825 8/8

15 / DOLL

Germany, early 20th century
Marked: Halbig Kämmer & Rein-
hardt 13, H 13 cm
Head in porcelain, glass eyes,
closed mouth, painted eye
brows, blond wig.
Body and limbs in composition, moveable.
Clothing: cotton underclothes,
batiste dress with lace, bonnet with lace, pearl necklace,
painted shoes and socks.
VM 64.57.148

pg. 54:

16 / GIRLS DOLL

Germany, early 20th century
Marked: Heinrich Handwerk/
Simon & Halbig, Germany 4,
H 64 cm
Porcelain head, brown glass
sleeping eyes, open mouth
with teeth, painted eye
brows and eye lashes, earrings in both ears, woollen
wig.
Body and limbs in wood.
Clothing: cotton underclothes,
red dress, cotton socks,
imitation leather shoes.
VM 89.75.10

pg. 55:

17 / DOLL, MILK MAID

Germany, early 20th century
Marked: Germany Heinrich
Handwerk Simon & Halbig,
H 50 cm
Porcelain head, blue glass
sleeping eyes, open mouth
with teeth, painted eye
brows and eye lashes,
pierced ears, wig with plait
in a bun.
Body and limbs in composi-
tion.
Clothing: cotton underclothes,
red/white striped cotton
skirt, red/purple striped
woollen over skirt, blue cotton blouse with white print,
white apron, scarf, lace bonnet, wooden clogs, with
copper milk churn.
VM 91.49.1

18

18 / DOLL

Germany, early 20th century
Marked: Steiff (stud in ear),
H 48 cm
Completely in felt filled with
straw.
Head with attached ears,
sewn mouth, black button
eyes, seam through the
middle of the face.
Clothing: fine cotton spotted
dress, batiste collar and bonnet.
VM 92.63.2

19 / DOLL

Germany, early 20th century
Marked: Steiff (stud in ear),
H 49 cm
Completely in felt filled with
straw.
Head with attached ears,
sewn mouth, eyes made
from black buttons, beard
and hair sewn on, seam
through the middle of the
face.
Clothing: cotton suit with sai-
lors collar, felt boots.
VM 92.63.15

20

20 / GIRLS DOLL

Germany, early 20th century
Marked: Made in Germany 11,
H 76 cm
Porcelain head, blue sleeping
eyes, open mouth with teeth,
painted eye brows and eye
lashes, synthetic hair in two
plaits.
Body in leather, jointed, porcelain lower arms and hands.
Clothing: cotton underclothes
with broderie and lace, long
sleeved dress in white/
yellow vichy checks, plastic
shoes.
VM 61.69.1 9/9

---

marked French dolls

21 / GIRLS DOLL

Germany, late 19th
early-20th century
Marked: 261. dep. Made in Ger-
many, H 39 cm
Porcelain head, glass eyes,
open mouth with teeth,
painted eye brows and eye
lashes, blond wig.
Body in composition, limbs
in wood.
Clothing: cotton underclothing, pink knitted woollen
dress and crochet beret, light
blue bead necklace, leather
shoes.
VM 92.63.11

23

pg. 60:

23 / GIRLS DOLL

France, late 19th century
Marked: on head: 4
on back: Jumeau Médaille d'Or
Paris, H 37 cm
Porcelain head, glass eyes,
closed mouth, painted eye
brows and eye lashes, wig
missing.
Body and limbs in composition, ball and socket joints.
Clothing: cotton underclothes,
dress in pink vichy check
with dropped waist, flounce
on skirt, red vichy hat with
bordeaux bow.
VM 58.53.9

pg. 61:

24 / GIRLS DOLL

France, circa 1880-85
Marked: on head: Déposé Tête
Jumeau / Bte SGDG 8
on body: Jumeau Médaille d'Or
Paris, H 48 cm
Porcelain head, glass eyes,
open mouth, painted eye
brows and eye lashes, real
hair wig.
Body and limbs in composition, hinged joints. Speaks
via mechanism in side: two
holes with cords to make doll
speak.
Clothing: cotton underclothes
with lace, short sleeved floral
dress, matching bonnet, silk
socks, imitation leather
shoes.
VM 61.88.1 4/4

25 / DOLL

France, 1888-1890
Marked: on head: Déposé E 25
(J), (= Emile Jumeau)
on back: Jumeau Médaille d'Or
Paris, H 28 cm
Porcelain head, glass eyes,
closed mouth, painted eye
brows and eye lashes, real
hair blond wig with luxu-
rious curls.
Body and limbs in wood
with joints.
Clothing: cotton underclothes,
batiste jacket bordered with
lace, cotton socks, leather
shoes.
This doll comes with a won-
derful sliding wardrobe with
mirror, a number of different
pieces of clothing, including,
2 petticoats, lace skirt, long
silk coat and matching hat, a
dark red dress, hair brush,
mattress and pillows.
VM 89.75.8 13/13

26

27

26 / GIRLS DOLL

France, late 19th century
Marked: on body: Jumeau
Médaille d'Or Paris, H 35 cm
Porcelain head, glass eyes,
closed mouth, blond hair
wig.
Body and limbs in composi-
tion.

Clothing: cotton underclothes,
woollen dress with satin
panels, long sleeved velvet
jacket, straw hat with large
bow.
VM 62.73.1

27 / GIRLS DOLL

France, 1889-1892
Marked on the head: J. Steiner Bte
S.G.D.G.
on the loins: Le Petit Parisien
Bébé. J.Steiner Marque Déposée
Médaille d'or 1889 Paris,
H 96 cm
Head in porcelain with big
blue sleeping eyes that move
with a handel behind the ear,

closed mouth, painted eyebrows and eyelashes, pierced
ears, real hair wig.
Body and limbs in composition, jointed.
Clothing: cotton underclothes,
checked cotton dress with
apron, leather boots with
buttons.
VM 92.63.51

65

28

28 / DOLL

France, early 20th century

Marked: SFBJ 301 Paris (Société Francaise de Fabrication de Bébés & Jouets), H 13 cm

Porcelain head, glass sleeping eyes, open mouth with teeth, mohair wig.

Body and limbs in composition, moveable.

Clothing: Blue silk dress with red bows, neck scarf, batiste apron, bonnet with lace, crucifix around neck, painted socks and shoes.

VM 64.57.149, (HH 428)

29 / COSTUME DOLL

France, early 20th century

Marked: Unis France 71 149 60, H 34 cm

Porcelain head, glass sleeping eyes, open mouth with teeth, painted eye brows and eye lashes, mohair wig.

Body and limbs in wood, jointed.

Clothing: cotton underclothing, felt dress decorated with gold and silver braid, lace collar, tulle apron decorated with beads, cotton socks, imitation leather shoes.

VM 70.30.15

30

pg. 68:

30 / COSTUME DOLL

France, early 20th century
Marked: Unis France 71 149 60,
H 35 cm
Porcelain head, glass sleeping
eyes, open mouth with teeth,
painted eye brows and eye
lashes, mohair wig.
Body in composition, limbs
in wood, jointed.
Clothing: white pleated woollen trousers, embroidered
blue velvet jacket, gaiters,
imitation leather shoes.
VM 70.30.16

1916 exhibition

pg. 69:

31 / GIRLS DOLL

France, circa 1883
Marked: on head: II,
on body: Jumeau /Médaille d'Or
/ Paris, named Bébé Jumeau,
H 60 cm
Porcelain head, glass eyes,
closed mouth, painted eye
lashes and eye brows, blond
mohair wig, gold coloured
ear rings.
Body and limbs in composition, jointed.
Clothing: cotton underclothes,
light green dress with woven
stripes, light yellow blouse,
light green coat with large
collar bordered with lace,
beret, gloves, cotton socks,
leather shoes.
With poster as a diploma for
participating in the exhibition in Antwerp in 1916.
VM 92.63.19

1934 exhibition

32 / PAGES

Germany, early 20th century
Marked: Knoch Gebrüder. Made in
Germany 201 13/0, H 28 cm
Head in porcelain with blue
sleeping eyes, open mouth
with teeth, painted eye-
brows, wig in smyrna.
Body and limbs in composition.
Clothing: suit in gaberdine
with felt vest, felt hat, leather
boots. Figures from the Antwerp procession.
VM 7992 – 7993

33 / PAGE

early 20th century
Unmarked, H 28 cm
Completely in composition.
Head with glass eyes, open
mouth, painted eyebrows
and eye lashes, wig in
smyrna.
Clothing: Trousers and vest in
green velvet with wide
sleeves, black cotton socks,
leather shoes, green velvet
cap. Figure from the Ant-
werp procession.
VM 7990

34 / SQUIRE

early 20th century
Unmarked, H 28 cm
Completely in composition.
Head with brown glass eyes,
open mouth with teeth,
painted eyebrows and eyelashes, wig in smyrna.
Clothing: beige suit with knickerbockers, brown velvet
vest with leather belt, brown
velvet cap, leather boots, and
quiver.
VM 7994

35 / FISHERMAN

early 20th century
Unmarked, H 28 cm
Completely in composition.
Head with brown glass eyes,
open mouth, painted eye-
brows and eyelashes.
Clothing: suit in coarse linen
with black buttons, leather
sou'wester and boots. Figure
from the Antwerp proces-
sion.
VM 7991

32

33

34

35

36

pg. 72:

36 / CAMP-FOLLOWER
early 20th century
Unmarked, H 24 cm
Head in celluloid, painted
eyes, mouth with teeth and
eyebrows.
Body and limbs in cloth, felt
hands.
Clothing: light blue felt skirt,
dark blue jacket with leather
belt, cotton apron, lacquer
hat with a rosette in the Belgian colours, black wooden
shoes with gaiters, a bottle in
the hand and small brandy
cask on a leather strap.
VM 9755

pg. 32:

**37 / THE VIRGIN OF
ANTWERP**
Germany, early 20th century
Marked: Heubach-Koppelsdorf
312 Sur 6 Germany, H 74 cm
Porcelain head, glass eyes,
open mouth with teeth, real
eyelashes, wig with long
blond plaits decorated with
flowers.
Body and limbs in composition with ball and socket
joints.
Clothing: underclothes in cotton and silk, long silk dress
with train, embroidered brocade corsage decorated with
the arms of Antwerp, shoes
in imitation leather.
VM 10.100

pg. 73:

38 / PAGES
Germany 19th – 20th century.
Marked: Heubach-Koppelsdorf
342 4/0, Germany, H 37 cm
Head in porcelain with glass
sleeping eyes, open mouth
with teeth, real hair wig cut
in page style.
Body and limbs in composition.
Clothing: Page suit in beige
velvet with batiste and lace
collar, velvet shoes, with a
little pillow in their hands.
VM 10.124-10.125

39 / ORNAMENTAL DOLL
20th century,
Unmarked, H 50 cm
Head in pressed cloth, painted eyes, closed mouth,
woollen wig.
Cloth body with composition
limbs.
Clothing: cotton underclothes,
grey silk dress, fine silk over-
dress decorated with silver
thread and lace, cloth hat,
painted shoes.
VM 10.128

40

42

43

pg.76:

40 / FASHION DOLL

1934

Unmarked, H 47 cm

Head in pressed cloth, painted eyes and mouth, woollen wig, straw hat with silk bow.

Body in cloth, limbs in stoneware.

Clothing: 1830's style dress, striped silk decorated with lace and bows, batiste underclothes, silk socks and leather shoes.

VM 10.141

pg.77:

41 / ORNAMENTAL DOLL

circa 1934

Unmarked, H 50 cm

Head in pressed cloth, painted eyes, mouth and eye brows, blond hair wig with ringlets.

Body and limbs in cloth, arms in stoneware.

Clothing: fashion anno 1850, cotton underclothes, purple silk dress with flounce, lace bodice, black shoes.

VM 10.142

42 / ORNAMENTAL DOLL

circa 1934

Unmarked, H 45 cm

Head in pressed cloth, painted eyes and mouth, woollen wig.

Body and limbs in cloth, lower arms and legs in composition.

Clothing: 19th century fashion, cotton underclothing, silk dress decorated with green prints and lace, tulle gloves, painted shoes, straw hat.

VM 10.127

43 / ORNAMENTAL DOLL

1934

Unmarked, H 32 cm

Head in pressed cloth, painted eyes and mouth, black wavy hair.

Body and limbs in cloth.

Clothing: circa 1850's fashion, cotton underclothes, velvet dress, lace frill and cuffs, lace bonnet with ostrich feathers, imitation leather shoes.

VM 10.137

44

49

pg.80:

44 / ORNAMENTAL DOLL

circa 1934

Unmarked, H 32 cm

Head in pressed cloth, painted eyes and mouth, white curly hair.
Body and limbs in cloth.
Clothing: circa 1860's fashion, cotton underclothes, black silk dress decorated with bows, damask bodice, white lace sleeves, lace bonnet, imitation leather shoes.
VM 10.132

pg.81:

45 / ORNAMENTAL DOLL

circa 1934

Unmarked, H 32 cm

Head in pressed cloth, painted eyes and mouth, woollen wig.
Body and limbs in cloth.
Clothing: circa 1870's fashion, cotton underclothes, dark yellow damask dress with flowers decorated with a black bow, black panels, lace shawl, imitation leather shoes, hat.
VM 10.131

pg.82:

46 / FASHION DOLL

1934

Unmarked, H 40 cm

Head in wax with painted eyes and mouth, woollen wig.
Body and legs in cloth, wax arms.
Clothing: dress in silver coloured synthetic material, red velvet cape, silver coloured hat, textile shoes.
VM 10.143

50

pg.83:

48 / ORNAMENTAL DOLL

circa 1934

Unmarked, H 46 cm

Head in pressed cloth with painted eyes and mouth, brown wig.
Body and limbs in cloth and stoneware.
Clothing: woollen skirt and jacket, decorative apron and shawl in muslin, velvet bonnet, parasol, moulded and painted shoes.
VM 10.139

49 / ARABIAN DANÇER

circa 1934

Unmarked: H 49 cm

Head in pressed cloth, gold coloured, painted eyes and mouth, black wig.
Body and limbs in cloth.
Clothing: red velvet blouse, gold brocade trousers with wide legs, long pointed bonnet, velvet shoes.
VM 10.170

50 / COSTUME DOLL

circa 1934

Unmarked, H 63 cm

Celluloid head, with sleeping eyes, open mouth with teeth, blond wig in plaits.
Body and limbs in leather and composition.

Clothing: Scandinavian costume: cotton underclothes, woollen embroidered skirt and apron, satin waistcoat, white cotton blouse, hat, imitation leather shoes.
Doll donated by Queen Astrid for the 1934 exhibition.
VM 10.095

51

51 / DOLL

circa 1934
Unmarked, H 62 cm
Celluloid head, painted eyes,
closed mouth, light brown
curly wig.
Cloth body and limbs.
Clothing: costume: red felt
pleated skirt with decorative
edges, waistcoat in velvet
decorated with sequins and
embroidered flowers, white
cotton blouse, bodice, satin
head scarf, embroidered satin
apron.
Doll donated by the Queen
of Italy for the 1934 exhibition.
VM 10.094

52 / COSTUME DOLL

circa 1934.
Unmarked, H 50 cm
Head in pressed cloth, painted eyes and mouth.
Body and legs in cloth, stoneware arms.
Clothing: cotton under clothes, quilted cotton skirt,
striped apron decorated with
flowers, red blouse, black
shawl with velvet bows,
clogs, white bonnet.
VM 92.63.13

53 / COSTUME DOLL

circa 1934

Unmarked, H 37 cm

Head in pressed cloth, painted eyes and mouth, blond wig.

Body and legs in cloth, stoneware lower arms.

Clothing: cotton underclothes with lace, black velvet dress, corsage decorated with beads, colourful apron, silk socks, headscarf decorated with lace bow, synthetic clogs, bead necklace.

VM 10.135

DOLLS AS MODELS

religious dolls

pg. 90:

54 / NUN

mid 19th century

Unmarked, H 45.5 cm

Head in composition with brown glass eyes, painted mouth and eyebrows.

Body, upper arms and legs in cloth, lower arms and hands in leather.

Clothing: black linen petticoat, faded black linen pinafore dress (appears green/brown), white linen collar and head scarf with black hood, rosary beads around the waist.

VM 60.9.180

pg. 91:

55 / NUN

mid 19th century

Unmarked, H 38 cm

Head and torso in composition, glass eyes, closed mouth painted eyebrows and hair. Upper body in cloth, lower body and limbs in leather.

Clothing: cotton underclothes; long black dress with apron, large collar and hood in batiste, rosary on belt, leather shoes.

VM 10.054

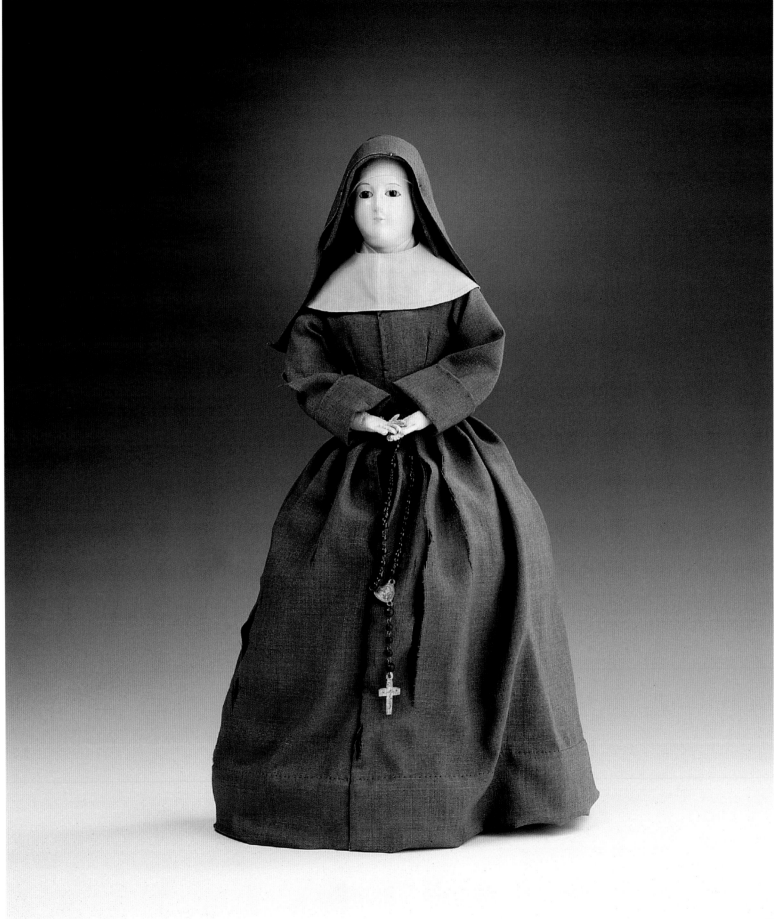

54

56

dolls in national costume and work clothing

56 / SOUVENIR DOLL

early 20th century
Unmarked, H 34 cm
Head in composition, black glass eyes, closed mouth, black hair in Japanese style. Body and limbs in composition.
Clothing: Japanese costume. Long embroidered trousers, embroidered silk dress – side closing; high platform shoes, head dress-painted metal bound with silk.
VM 10.169

57 / BLACK DOLL

19th-20th century
Unmarked, H 11,5 cm
Completely in porcelain with black glaze, white eyes.
Clothing: diverse felt petticoats; felt skirt decorated with beads, pearl necklace.
VM 8286

58

58 / SOLDIER

19th century
Unmarked, H 24 cm
Head in composition, with painted eyes, mouth, moustache and hair.
Body in composition, limbs in cloth.

Clothing: officers uniform of the Austrian Imperial Guard, white felt trousers, red felt jacket with gold coloured piping and braid, high black paper boots, silver coloured metal helmet with feathers, metal sable.
VM 9809

pg. 94:

59 / FARMERS WIFE

20th century
Unmarked, H 56 cm
Head in composition, painted eyes and mouth, modelled and painted hair. Body and limbs in leather, cloth lower limbs.
Clothing: cotton and felt underclothes, cotton dress and apron, floral shawl, lace bonnet, wooden clogs.
VM 9749

pg. 95:

60 / PEG WOODEN DOLL

Germany: Grödnertal, 19th century
Unmarked, H 32cm
Head and chest in wood, painted eyes, mouth, eye brows and hair. Cloth body and legs, wooden arms.
Clothing: Dutch costume. Cotton dress with lace collar, broderie apron, bonnet in tulle and lace, two metal curlers under the bonnet.
VM 92.63.46

pg. 96:

61 / PEG WOODEN DOLL

Germany: Grödnertal, late 19th century
Unmarked, H 31 cm
Head and torso in wood, painted eyes, mouth and hair.
Cloth body and legs, lower arms in wood.
Clothing: stiff petticoat, cotton dress with light blue pattern, lace collar and sleeves, checked apron, lace bonnet with typical metal curlers.
VM 92.63.34

pg. 97:

62 / PEG WOODEN DOLL

Germany: Grödnertal, late 19th century
Unmarked, H 30 cm
Head and torso in wood, painted eyes, mouth and hair.
Cloth body and legs, lower arms in wood.
Clothing: cotton dress with blue floral motif, black apron with white motif, gold coloured decorations on bodice, lace bonnet with typical metal plates.
VM 92.63.47

61

63

64

63 / COSTUME DOLL

20th century

Unmarked, H 18 cm

Wire frame, covered with
wool.

Head with sewn eyes and
mouth, woollen wig.

Clothing: felt dress with velvet
border, damask apron, broderie headdress, velvet shoes.

VM 9831

**64 / PEG WOODEN DOLL:
FARMERS WIFE**

late 19th century

*Unmarked: Grödnertal type,
H 25 cm*

Completely in wood, head
with painted eyes, mouth
and hair.

Clothing: woollen petticoat,
black/white checked cotton
dress, apron, woollen coat
with hood, velvet bonnet.

VM 4493

65   66   67

**65 / PEG WOODEN DOLL:
SACK CARRIER**

late 19th century
Unmarked: Grödnertal type,
H 24 cm
Completely in wood, head
with painted eyes, mouth,
moustache and hair.
Clothing: cotton trousers,
smock in waxed cotton, cot-
ton cap, wooden shoes.
VM 9783

**66 / PEG WOODEN DOLL:
POLICEMAN**

late 19th century
Unmarked: Grödnertal type,
H 26.5 cm
Completely in wood, head
with painted eyes, mouth,
moustache and hair.
Clothing: felt uniform, leather
belt, felt cap with leather
brim.
VM 4471

**67 / PEG WOODEN DOLL:
LADY**

late 19th century
Unmarked: Grödnertal type,
H 24 cm
Completely in wood, head
with painted eyes, mouth
and hair.
Clothing: silk dress, shawl
bordered with tassels and
pearls, metal necklace with
cross, earrings.
VM 9795

**68 / PEG WOODEN DOLL:
BISHOP**

late 19th century
Unmarked: Grödnertal type,
H 29 cm
Completely in wood, head
with painted eyes and
mouth.
Clothing: purple woollen
gown, cotton alb with lace,
red velvet chasuble finished
with gold thread, velvet
mitre decorated with gold
thread, copper staff.
VM 9789

101

69

70

69 / PEG WOODEN DOLL: PRIEST

late 19th century
Unmarked: Grödnertal type,
H 24 cm
Completely in wood, head
with painted eyes, mouth
and hair.
Clothing: felt underpants, felt
soutane with buttons, scarf as
belt, train, felt hat.
VM 9788

70 / PEG WOODEN DOLL

Germany, 20th century
Unmarked: Grödnertal,
H 10.5 cm
Completely in wood, head
with painted eyes, mouth
and hair.
Clothing: velvet suit, striped
scarf, flat cotton hat.
VM 9839

character dolls

71 / CHARACTER DOLL

20th century
Unmarked, H 67 cm
Head in pressed cloth filled
with straw, painted eyes,
mouth and wrinkles, white
woollen wig.
Body and limbs in cloth, sto-

neware hands.
Clothing: cotton underclothes,
purple woollen long sleeved
dress, satin apron and scarf,
lace bonnet, glasses, socks
and wooden clogs.
VM 92.63.1

72

pg. 104:

72 / FARMERS WIFE

20th century

Unmarked, H 56 cm

Completely in wood. Well carved head and hands, painted eyes, mouth and hair.

Upper body formed in plaster.

Clothing: cotton underclothes, red striped skirt, cotton blouse, linen apron, neck and head scarf, wooden clogs carved into the legs.

VM 10.103

pg. 105:

73 / ORNAMENTAL DOLL

20th century

Unmarked, H 82 cm

Completely in cloth. Head with painted eyes and mouth, wig with long blond plaits.

Hands in composition.

Clothing: cotton underclothes with wide lace, long silk gown decorated with silver braid and set with pearls, artificial precious stones and heart shaped metal decoration, bolero finished with imitation fur, cotton sleaves with embroidery and lace, headdress in same material as dress, silver coloured, decorated with pearls and loops with small pearls, leather boots.

VM 10.096

74 / DOLL

early 20th century

Unmarked, H 25 cm

Completely in cloth filled with straw. Head with drawn features, mouth, eyes and wrinkles, large nose attached, woollen wig.

Clothing: cotton blouse and apron, crepe skirt, shoes sewn on. Represents an old woman or witch.

VM 9753

75

75 / SWADDLING CLOTHED DOLL

Germany, 19th century
Unmarked, H 23.5 cm
Completely in wood. Head with painted eyes, mouth and hair.
Body painted with flowers.
VM 5300

76 / SWADDLING CLOTHED DOLL

Germany, 19th century
Unmarked, H 30.5 cm
Completely in wood. Head with painted eyes, mouth and hair.
Body painted with flowers.
VM 5485

76

77

77 / SWADDLING CLOTHED DOLL

Germany, 19th century.
Unmarked, H 7,5 cm
Completely in wood, swaddling clothed doll in rocking crib, painted decoration.
VM 92.63.35

FUNCTIONAL DOLLS

pg. 110:
78 / MUSICIAN

late 18th – early 19th century?
Unmarked, H 32 cm
Head in wood, painted eyes and mouth, fur wig.
Body and limbs in wire frame covered with hemp. Wooden fore arms and hands.
Clothing: red jacket, waistcoat edged with gold braid, lace jabot, knee breeches, brown velvet cocked hat, paper socks. The cymbals in his hands work via a mechanism in the back.
VM 92.63.14

pg. 111:
79 / MUSICAL AUTOMATON: BOY

France, late 18th century
Unmarked, H & G Vichy (?),
H 48.5 cm L 27 cm B 18.5 cm
Head in composition, with open mouth, painted teeth, brown glass eyes, real hair.
Body in wood and papier-maché. Lower arms and hands in porcelain and wood.
Clothing: black velvet knee breeches, black velvet jumper with polo neck, green and white knitted jumper (not original), metal cap with ass's ears covered with piece of cardboard that bears the inscription ANE, brown silk socks, black leather shoes, originally had a book with the alphabet in one hand (lost), figure seated on a bench.
VM 90.3.3

pg. 112:
80 / MUSICAL AUTOMATON: GIRL

France, late 19th century
Unmarked, H & G Vichy (?),
H 48 cm L 27 cm B 18.5 cm
Head in composition, with open mouth, painted teeth, brown glass eyes, real hair.
Body in wood and papier-maché. Lower arms and hands in porcelain.
Clothing: cotton underclothes with a broad lace border, black velvet skirt, green and white knitted jumper and bonnet (not original), brown silk socks, black leather shoes, apple in one hand, figure seated on a bench.
VM 90.3.2.

pg. 113:
81 / MAROT

France (?), late 19th century
Unmarked, H 36 cm
Head in porcelain with glass eyes, closed mouth, painted eye brows and eye lashes.
The body is composed of a cardboard ball with a mechanism on a wooden stick to make music.
Clothing: fools clothes in satin (green/orange) with bells, fools cap also with bells.
VM 92.63.32

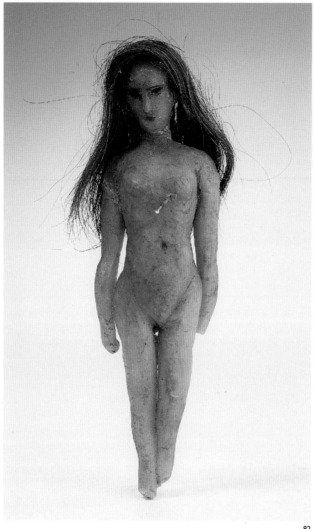

82

dolls with diverse functions

82 / DOLL
19th-20th century
Unmarked, H 16 cm
Completely in wax. Head
with slightly open mouth,
black painted eyes, real hair.
Body completely modeled in
female form. With a pin pushed through her heart. Used
when casting a spell, a magic
practice where death or dis-
ease is wished upon the vic-
tim, from a distance.
VM 4920

83 / LAY FIGURE
18th-19th century
Unmarked, H 48 cm
Completely in wood, with
movable ball and socket
joints. The doll was used as a
model for drawing practice.
VM 60.59.33

pg. 116:

84 / ORNAMENTAL DOLL BON-BON BOX: FRANCE

late 19th century

Doll unmarked. H 42 cm

Mark on box: Boissier Confiseur 7B. des Capucines Paris, Head in porcelain with glass eyes, closed mouth, painted eye lashes and eye brows, ear rings, blond wig.

Body consists of a cardboard box, arms and legs in porcelain.

Clothing: cotton underclothes, silk skirt with lace and beads, velvet jacket, lace shall, parasol, leather shoes.

VM 60.9.254 a

pg. 117:

86 / COLLECTION BOX

early 20th century

Unmarked, H 49 cm

Head in composition, glass eyes, open mouth with teeth. Body and legs formed by a metal collection box upon which the head is placed, wooden arms. The back has a handel covered in red material.

Clothing: cotton underclothes, black silk skirt, red velvet jacket with batiste collar, felt hat.

VM 63.7.1.

87 / TEA COSY

20th century

Unmarked, H 42 cm

Head in pressed felt with filling, white wig with pony tail, painted eyes and mouth. Arms and hands in felt. Body formed by a tea cosy in felt, thick swanskin layer.

Clothing: red coachman's jacket with jabot, whip in hand.

VM 92.63.31

88 / NEAPOLITAN CHRISTMAS CRIB DOLL: BLACK KING

Italy
Unmarked, H 35 cm
Head and torso in terracotta, handmodelled, expressive face, negroid, with painted brown eyes, mouth and curly hair.
Body partly in hemp, limbs in wood, red painted boots.
Clothing: linen knickerbockers, silk jacket decorated with gold plated sequins, waistband, red silk coat, blue overcoat with brocade train, edges decorated with sequins, wide yellow collar.
VM 55.2.22

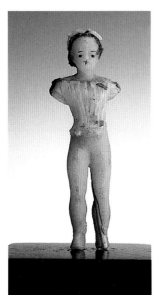
89

89 / DOLL

late 19th – early 20th century.
Unmarked, H 7 cm
Completely in wax, strengthened with wooden sticks and attached to a metal pole. Head, body and limbs modelled, eyes and mouth painted. Probably used as a cake decoration.
VM 92.63.58

pg. 122:

90 / GIRLS DOLL

late 19th century
Unmarked; H 37 cm
Porcelain head, glass eyes, closed mouth, painted eye brows and eye lashes, blond real hair wig with red satin bows.
Body and limbs in wood.
Clothing: cotton and flannel underclothes, felt skirt, woollen corsage, satin bonnet with lace border.
VM 58.53.7

pg. 123:

91 / GIRLS DOLL

late 19th-early 20th century
Unmarked, H 44 cm
Porcelain head, glass eyes, closed mouth, painted eye brows and eye lashes, blond woollen wig.
Body and limbs in wood.
Clothing: cotton underclothes, floral dress with pleated skirt and sailor collar, leather shoes.
VM 54.38.1

pg. 124:

92 / GIRLS DOLL

France (?), 1870-1890
Unmarked: J.Steiner (?),
H 45 cm
Head in porcelain, glass eyes, open mouth with teeth, real hair wig.
Body and legs in leather and composition, wooden arms, ball and socket joints. Walking mechanism wound up with a key.
Clothing: original cotton underclothes, cotton dress with dropped waist, skirt in broderie, silk socks, leather shoes.
VM 60.88.12.

pg. 125:

93 / BABY DOLL: 'ROOZEKE'

2nd half 19th century
Unmarked, H 27 cm
Head in composition, moveable glass eyes, closed mouth, painted hair.
Body and hands in composition, limbs in wood.
Clothing: cotton and flannel underclothes, long christening gown decorated with ribbons and bows, bonnet; extra baby clothes.
VM 60.9.168

94

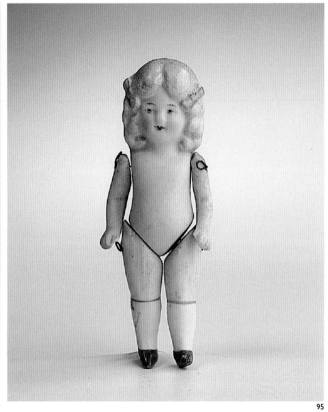

95

94 / BOYS DOLL

early 20th century

Unmarked, H 10.5 cm

Completely in porcelain, closed mouth, painted eyes, modelled and coloured hair. Moveable arms.

Clothing: painted onto the porcelain: cardigan, knickerbockers, socks, shoes and cap.

VM 87.25.6

95 / GIRLS DOLL

early 20th century

Unmarked, H 10.5 cm

Completely in porcelain, closed mouth, painted eyes, modelled blond curly hair. Moveable arms and legs.

Clothing: painted white socks and shoes.

VM 87.25.8

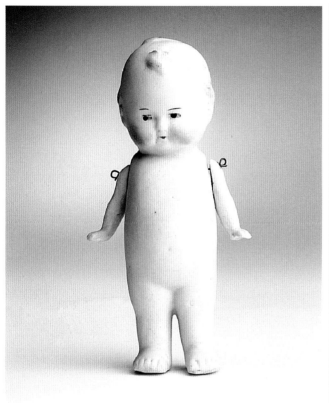

96

97

96 / BABY DOLL

early 20th century

Marked: 701 (on back),

H 11 cm

Completely in porcelain,

painted eyes and mouth,

modelled blond hair.

Body with large belly.

No clothing.

VM 92.63.33

97 / GIRLS DOLL

19th – 20th century

Unmarked, H 22 cm

Completely in porcelain.

Head with glass eyes, open

mouth with teeth, painted

eyebrows and eyelashes,

woollen wig.

Clothing: cotton underclothes,

pink checked cotton dress

with short sleeves, broderie

on the neck, ribbon with

bow, painted socks and

shoes.

VM 54.38.2

127

98

98 / GIRLS DOLL
19th-20th century
Unmarked, H 14 cm
Porcelain head, sleeping
eyes, opened mouth with
teeth, painted eyebrows and
eye lashes, woollen wig.
Body and limbs in composition.
Clothing: cotton underclothes,
light blue dress with matching muff, painted shoes
and socks.
VM 59.14.820

99 / CLOWN
late 19th-early 20th century
Unmarked, H 49 cm
Completely in papier-maché,
painted mouth, eyes, eye
brows and hair.
Clothing: papier-maché hat,
two colour cotton clowns
suit bordered with lace:
second suit in different
colours.
VM 59.14.818

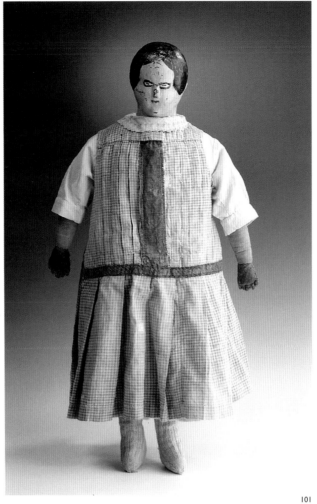

101

100 / RAG DOLL

USA, early 20th century
Marked: Art Fabric Mills/ Paten-
ted/ Feb. 13-1900, H 58 cm
Completely in cotton with
painted eyes, hair, mouth
and hands.
Clothing: cotton and wool
underclothes with corset for
children, cotton dress, apron
with frill, cotton socks.
VM 89.75.11

101 / DOLL

19th century
Unmarked, H 62 cm
Completely in wood, solid
wood head and torso, painted eyes, mouth and hair.
Body and limbs in cloth, filled, leather hands
Clothing: cotton and flannel
underclothes, white cotton
dress, blue/white checked
cotton apron with a wide
skirt, cotton socks.
VM 92.63.5

102 / GIRLS DOLL

Belgium, circa 1970
Marked: Unica Belgium,
H 48 cm
Completely in plastic. Head with blue sleeping eyes, open mouth, implanted nylon blond hair.
Clothing: cotton underclothes, blue and white cotton check dress, white blouse, white plastic shoes.
VM 88.52.1

104

106

METHODS OF DOLL
MANUFACTURING

hand made dolls

103 / SWADDLING CLOTHED DOLL

Belgium, 19th century
Unmarked, H 20 cm
Modeled from a square piece of clay. Simple head form, doll in swaddling clothes, simple decoration.
VM 4642

104 / SWADDLING CLOTHED DOLL

Belgium, 19th century
Unmarked, H 16.5 cm
Modeled from a square piece of clay. Simple head form, doll in swaddling clothes, simple decoration.
VM 4643

pg. 134:

105 / DOLL

19th – 20th century
Unmarked, H 29 cm
Completely in wood.
Simple doll with movable arms, rough finish. The eyes are formed by two nails.
VM nr 4841

106 / DOLL

20th century
Unmarked, H 42 cm
Plaited from one strand of hemp, consists of a head with hair in french plait, body with arms.
VM 4646

pg. 135:

107 / DOLL

20th century
Unmarked, H 37 cm
Plaited from one strand of hemp, the eyes and mouth are marked with metal pins.
VM 4651

103

105

108

109

108 / DOLL

20th century

Unmarked, H 56 cm

Made from plaited straw:
head, body and legs from
one strand, a second strand
forms the arms.

VM 92.63.39

109 / DOLL

20th century

Unmarked, H 15 cm

Wire frame covered with
plaited straw: with skirt,
apron and hat.

VM 92.63.40

111   112

III / DOLL: TENNIS PLAYER

20th century.

Unmarked, H 16 cm

Wire frame, covered with
wool.

Head with sewn eyes and
mouth, brown woollen wig.

Clothing: white woollen
dress.

VM 9820

II2 / DOLLS: DANCING PAIR

20th century

Unmarked, H 7 cm

Wire frame bound with
wool.

Man: felt jacket and hat.

Woman: crochet skirt, silk
hair with a large silk bow.

VM 9824

138

115

---

dolls made by craftsmen

113 / DOLLS HEADS

19th century

Unmarked, H 7 cm

Series of wooden dolls heads, with torso, with painted grey and blue eyes, mouth, cheeks and black hair.

These dolls heads were made in large numbers and sold to people who made their own dolls.

VM 4430-4431, 5283-5292, 5294-5296, 5445-5418

115 / PEG WOODEN DOLL

Germany: Grödnertal, 19th century

Unmarked, H 41 cm

Head and shoulders in wood, painted eyes, mouth and hair.

Body and limbs in cloth, wooden fore arms.

Clothing: cotton underclothes, floral cotton dress with lace finish, yellow bows.

VM 92.63.29

141

119

pg. 140:

116 / PEG WOODEN DOLL

Germany: Grödnertal,
mid 19th century
Unmarked, H 32 cm
Head and shoulders in wood,
carved and painted eyes and
nose, modelled hair.
Cloth body and limbs, stoneware arms.
Clothing: cotton underclothes,
cotton dress with lace, boots
in waxed cotton.
VM 4654

pg. 141:

117 / POUPARD,
(CHUBBY BABY DOLL)

France (?), 19th century
Unmarked, H 27 cm
Head and shoulders in composition, painted eyes,
mouth eye-brows and hair.
Cardboard body, no legs,
wire arms with wooden
hands. Mechanism in back to
move arms.
Clothing: check cotton dress,
plain apron, bonnet in tulle.
VM 92.63.21

118 / POUPARD,
(CHUBBY BABY DOLL)

France (?), 19th century
Unmarked, H 18 cm
Completely in cardboard
covered with a lacquer layer.
Swaddling clothed doll. Head
with painted eyes, nose and
mouth.
Moveable arms with a bottle
in the hand.
Painted baby clothes and
bonnet.
VM 59.14.714

119 / POUPARD,
(CHUBBY BABY DOLL)

France (?), 19th century
Unmarked, H 24 cm
Completely in cardboard.
Head with painted eyes,
nose, mouth and hair.
Swaddling clothed doll.
VM 5901

143

120

industrially manufactured dolls

120 / DOLLS HEAD
Germany, early 20th century
Marked: SH 1079 -4 Dep Ger-
many (= Simon and Halbig),
H 8 cm
Porcelain head with blue
glass eyes, open mouth with
teeth, painted eye brows,
pierced ears, no wig.
VM 92.63.16

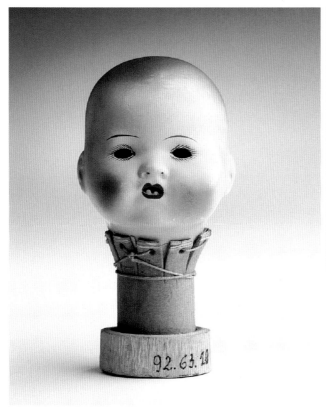

122

123

122 / DOLLS HEAD: BABIES HEAD

Germany, early 20th century
Marked: AM Armand Marseille,
H 11 cm
Porcelain head, blue glass
eyes, open mouth, painted
eye brows and hair. Stitched
neckpiece in cardboard.
VM 92.63.20

123 / DOLLS HEAD

mid 19th century
Marked: 26, H 7 cm
Head in bisque with torso,
closed mouth, painted eyes,
hair and cheeks.
VM 5460

145

125

124 / DOLL

late 19th-early 20th century
Marked: Dep 4, H 73 cm
Porcelain head with torso,
blue glass eyes, open mouth
with teeth, painted eye
brows, pierced ears, blond
woollen wig.
Body, upper arms and legs in
leather, porcelain lower
arms.
VM 92.63.24

125 / MOULD

Belgium, 20th century
Marked: Unica Belgium,
H 13.5 cm
Bronze head, part of a mould
used to make dolls heads.
VM 73.12.2

pg. 148:

126 / DOLL

Belgium, 20th century
Marked: Made in Belgium,
H 49 cm
Head in composition, sleeping eyes (eyes missing),
open mouth with teeth,
painted eye lashes and eye
brows.
Body and limbs in papier-
maché.
VM 92.63.9

147

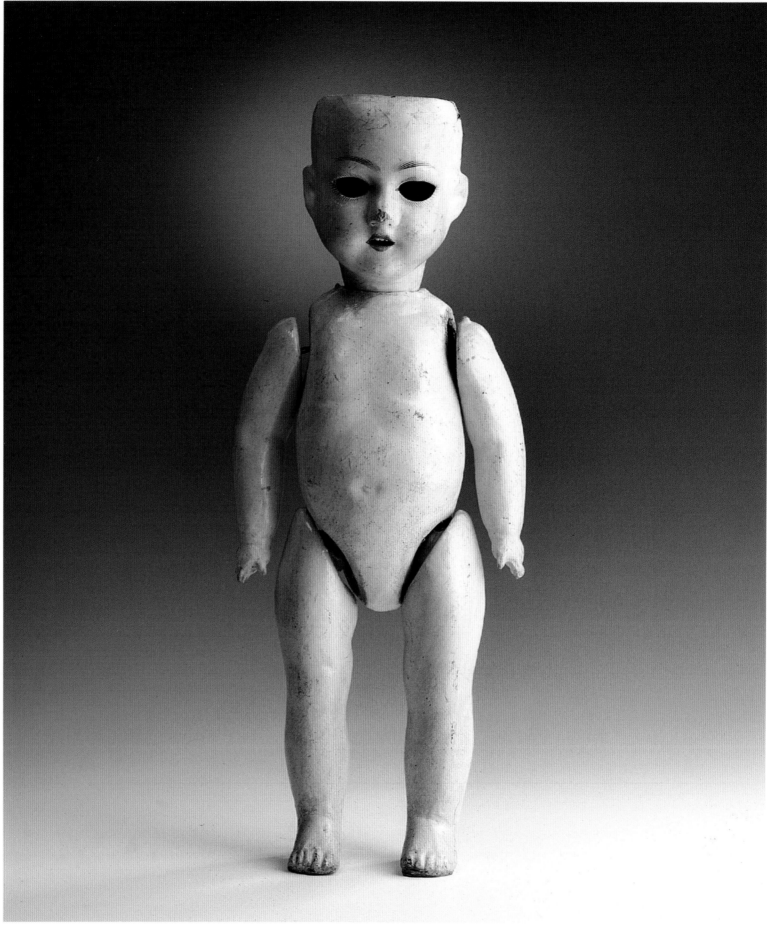

Catalogue

cat. 1, pg. 2
Baby doll: 'Margriet', Belgium,
early 18th century
Unmarked, h 67.5 cm,
VM 92.63.50

cat. 2, pg. 42
Bust, early 19th century
Unmarked, h 16cm,
VM 5561

cat. 3, pg. 42
Bust, early 19th century
Unmarked, h 18 cm,
VM 5459

cat. 4, pg. 43
Ornamental – fashion doll,
France (?), late 19th century
Unmarked, h 46cm,
VM 58.53.8

cat. 5, pg. 44
Ornamental – fashion doll,
France (?), late 19th century
Unmarked, h 44cm,
VM 9762

cat. 6, pg. 45
Girls doll, pre 1850
Unmarked, h 48cm,
VM 10.108

cat. 7, pg. 46
Peg wooden doll, Germany,
19th century
Unmarked: Grödnertal,
h 26.5 cm, VM 4487

cat. 8, pg. 46
Dolls, Germany, circa 1912
Marked: Heubach-Koppels-
dorff 250 19/0 Germany
h 16 cm, VM 5515-5516

cat. 9, pg. 47
Girls doll 'Reine de Saba', Germany, early 20th century.
Marked: Armand Marseille
390 A 4 M Made in Ger-
many, h 47 cm, VM 10.109

cat. 10, pg. 48
Bride, Germany, after 1894.
Marked 1894 Am 1 DEP
Made in Germany Armand
Marseille, h 38 cm,
VM 60.9.172

cat. 11, pg. 49
Baby doll, Germany, early
20th century
Marked: Armand Marseille
A.M. Germany 351 K,
h 23 cm, VM 89.75.9.

cat. 12, pg. 50
Twins, Germany, post 1890
Marked: Armand Marseille
390 7/10 Made in Germany,
h 31 cm, VM 92.63.36,
92.63.37

cat. 13, pg. 51
Character doll,
early 20th century
Marked: Kämmer & Rein-
hardt 30, h 31 cm,
VM 59.14.822

cat. 14, pg. 52
Character doll, Germany, early
20th century

Marked: on head: 149 5°, on
body: Kämmer & Reinhardt,
h 42 cm, VM 59.14.825 8/8

cat. 15, pg. 53
Doll, Germany,
early 20th century
Marked: Halbig Kämmer &
Reinhardt 13, h 13 cm,
VM 64.57.148

cat. 16, pg. 54
Girls doll, Germany,
early 20th century
Marked: Heinrich Hand-
werk/ Simon & Halbig, Germany 4, h 64 cm,
VM 89.75.10

cat. 17, pg. 55
Doll, Milk maid, Germany,
early 20th century
Marked: Germany Heinrich
Handwerk Simon & Halbig,
h 50 cm, VM 91.49.1

cat. 18, pg. 56
Doll, Germany,
early 20th century
Marked: Steiff (stud in ear),
h 48 cm, VM 92.63.2

cat. 19, pg. 57
Doll, Germany,
early 20th century
Marked: Steiff (stud in ear),
h 49 cm, VM 92.63.15

cat. 20, pg. 58
Girls doll, Germany,
early 20th century
Marked: Made in Germany
11, h 76 cm,
VM 61.69.1 9/9

cat. 21, pg. 59
Girls doll, Germany,
late 19th-early 20th century
Marked: 261. dep. Made in
Germany, h 39 cm,
VM 92.63.11

cat. 22, pg. 30
Girls doll, France,
late 19th century
Marked: on head: Dep. 10,
on body: Jumeau Médaille
d'Or Paris, h 51 cm
VM 58.53.6

cat. 23, pg. 60
Girls doll, France,
late 19th century
Marked: on head: 4, on
back: Jumeau Médaille d'Or
Paris, h 37cm
VM 58.53.9

cat. 24, pg. 61
Girls doll, France,
circa 1880-85
Marked: on head: Déposé
Tête Jumeau / Bte SGDG 8,
on body: Jumeau Médaille
d'Or Paris, h 48cm,
VM 61.88.1 4/4

cat. 25, pg. 63
Doll, France, 1888-1890
Marked: on head: Déposé E
25 (J), (= Emile Jumeau), on
back: Jumeau Médaille d'Or
Paris, h 28 cm,
VM 89.75.8 13/13

cat. 26, pg. 64
Girls doll, France,
late 19th century
Marked: on body: Jumeau
Médaille d'Or Paris, h 35 cm,
VM 62.73.1

cat. 27, pg. 65
Girls doll, France, 1889-1892
Marked on the head: J.
Steiner Bte S.G.D.G., on the
loins: Le Petit Parisien Bébé.
J.Steiner Marque Déposée
Médaille d'or 1889 Paris;
h 96 cm, VM 92.63.51

149

cat. 28, pg. 66
Doll, France, early 20th
century
Marked: SFBJ 301 Paris
(Société Francaise de Fab-
rication de Bébés & Jouets),
h 13 cm, VM 64.57.149,
(HH 428)

cat. 29, pg. 67
Costume doll, France,
early 20th century
Marked: Unis France 71 149
60, h 34 cm, VM 70.30.15

cat. 30, pg. 68
Costume doll, France,
early 20th century
Marked: Unis France 71 149
60, h 35 cm, VM 70.30.16

cat. 31, pg. 69
Girls doll, France, circa 1883
Marked: on head II,
on body: Jumeau /Médaille
d'Or / Paris, named Bébé
Jumeau, h 60 cm,
VM 92.63.19

cat. 32, pg. 71
Pages, Germany,
early 20th century
Marked: Knoch Gebrüder
Made in Germany 201 13/0,
h 28 cm, VM 7992 – 7993

cat. 33, pg. 71
Page, early 20th century
Unmarked, h 28 cm,
VM 7990

cat. 34, pg. 71
Squire, early 20th century
Unmarked, h 28 cm,
VM 7994

cat. 35, pg. 72
Fisherman, early 20th century
Unmarked, h 28 cm,
VM 7991

cat. 36, pg. 72
Camp-follower,
early 20th century
Unmarked, h 24 cm,
VM 9755

cat. 37, pg. 32
The Virgin of Antwerp, Germany, early 20th century
Marked: Heubach-Koppels-
dorf 312 Sur 6 Germany,
h 74 cm, VM 10.100

cat. 38, pg. 73
Pages, Germany 19th –
20th century.
Marked: Heubach-Koppels-
dorf 342 4/0, Germany,
h 37 cm, VM 10.124-10.125

cat. 39, pg. 75
Ornamental doll, 20th century,
Unmarked, h 50 cm,
VM 10.128

cat. 40, pg. 76
Fashion doll, 1934
Unmarked, h 47 cm,
VM 10.141

cat. 41, pg. 77
Ornamental doll, circa 1934
Unmarked, h 50 cm,
VM 10.142

cat. 42, pg. 78
Ornamental doll, circa 1934
Unmarked, h 45 cm,
VM 10.127

cat. 43, pg. 79
Ornamental doll, 1934
Unmarked, h 32 cm,
VM 10.137

cat. 44, pg. 80
Ornamental doll, circa 1934
Unmarked, h 32 cm,
VM 10.132

cat. 45, pg. 81
Ornamental doll, circa 1934
Unmarked, h 32 cm,
VM 10.131

cat. 46, pg. 82
Fashion doll, 1934
Unmarked, h 40 cm,
VM 10.143

cat. 47, pg. 19
Ornamental doll, circa 1934
Unmarked, h 43 cm,
VM 10.133

cat. 48, pg. 83
Ornamental doll, circa 1934
Unmarked, h 46 cm,
VM 10.139

cat. 49, pg. 84
Arabian dancer, circa 1934
Unmarked, h 49 cm,
VM 10.170

cat. 50, pg. 85
Costume doll, circa 1934
Unmarked, h 63 cm,
VM 10.095

cat. 51, pg. 86
Doll, circa 1934
Unmarked, h 62 cm,
VM 10.094

cat. 52, pg. 87
Costume doll, circa 1934.
Unmarked, h 50 cm,
VM 92.63.13

Cat 53, pg. 88
Costume doll, circa 1934
Unmarked, h 37 cm,
VM 10.135.

cat. 54, pg. 90
Nun, mid 19th century
Unmarked, h 45.5 cm,
VM 60.9.180

cat. 55, pg. 91
Nun, mid 19th century
Unmarked, h 38 cm,
VM 10.054

cat. 56, pg. 92
Souvenir doll,
early 20th century
Unmarked, h 34 cm,
VM 10.169

cat. 57, pg. 93
Black doll, 19th-20th century
Unmarked, h 11,5 cm,
VM 8286

cat. 58, pg. 93
Soldier, 19th century
Unmarked, h 24 cm,
VM 9809

cat. 59, pg. 94
Farmers wife, 20th century
Unmarked, h 56 cm,
VM 9749

cat. 60, pg. 95
Peg wooden doll, Germany:
Grödnertal, 19th century
Unmarked, h 32 cm,
VM 92.63.46

cat. 61, pg. 96
Peg wooden doll, Germany:
Grödnertal, late 19th century
Unmarked, h 31 cm,
VM 92.63.34

cat. 62, pg. 97
Peg wooden doll, Germany:
Grödnertal, late 19th century
Unmarked, h 30 cm,
VM 92.63.47

cat. 63, pg. 98
Costume doll, 20th century
Unmarked, h 18 cm,
VM 9831

cat. 64, pg. 99
Peg wooden doll: Farmers wife,
late 19th century
Unmarked: Grödnertal type,
h 25 cm, VM 4493

cat. 65, pg. 100
Peg wooden doll: sack carrier,
late 19th century
Unmarked: Grödnertal type,
h 24 cm, VM 9783

cat. 66, pg. 100
Peg wooden doll: policeman,
late 19th century
Unmarked: Grödnertal type,
h 26.5 cm, VM 4471

cat. 67, pg. 100
Peg wooden doll: Lady,
late 19th century
Unmarked: Grödnertal type,
h 24 cm, VM 9795

cat. 68, pg. 101
Peg wooden doll: Bishop,
late 19th century
Unmarked: Grödnertal type,
h 29 cm, VM 9789

cat. 69, pg. 102
Peg wooden doll: Priest,
late 19th century
Unmarked: Grödnertal type,
h 24 cm, VM 9788

cat. 70, pg. 102
Peg wooden doll, Germany,
20th century
Unmarked: Grödnertal,
h 10.5 cm, VM 9839

cat. 71, pg. 103
Character doll, 20th century
Unmarked, h 67 cm,
VM 92.63.1

cat. 72, pg. 104
Farmers wife, 20th century
Unmarked, h 56 cm,
VM 10.103

cat. 73, pg. 105
Ornamental doll, 20th century
Unmarked, h 82 cm,
VM 10.096

cat. 74, pg. 107
Doll, early 20th century
Unmarked, h 25 cm,
VM 9753

cat. 75, pg. 108
Swaddling clothed doll,
Germany, 19th century
Unmarked, h 23.5 cm,
VM 5300

cat. 76, pg. 109
Swaddling clothed doll,
Germany, 19th century
Unmarked, h 30.5 cm,
VM 5485

cat. 77, pg. 109
Swaddling clothed doll,
Germany, 19th century.
Unmarked, h 7,5 cm,
VM 92.63.35

cat. 78, pg. 110
Musician, late 18th – early
19th century?
Unmarked, h 32 cm,
VM 92.63.14

cat. 79, pg. 111
Musical automaton: Boy,
France, late 18th century
Unmarked, h & G Vichy (?),
h 48.5 cm, l 27 cm,
b 18.5 cm, VM 90.3.3

cat. 80, pg. 112
Musical automaton: Girl,
France, late 19th century
Unmarked, h & G Vichy (?),
h 48 cm, l 27 cm, b 18.5 cm,
VM 90.3.2.

cat. 81, pg. 113
Marot, France (?),
late 19th century
Unmarked, h 36 cm,
VM 92.63.32

cat. 82, pg. 114
Doll, 19th-20th century
Unmarked, h 16 cm,
VM 4920

cat. 83, pg. 115
Lay figure, 18th-19th century
Unmarked, h 48 cm,
VM 60.59.33

cat. 84, pg. 116
Ornamental doll bon-bon box,
France, late 19th century
Doll unmarked. h 42 cm,
Mark on box: Boissier Confi-
seur 7B. des Capucines Paris
VM 60.9.254 a

cat. 85, pg. 35
Ornamental doll bon-bon box,
France, late 19th century
Doll unmarked, h 42 cm,
Mark on box: Boissier Confi-
seur 7 B. des Capucines Paris
VM 60.9.254b

cat. 86, pg. 117
Collection box,
early 20th century
Unmarked, h 49 cm,
VM 63.7.1.

cat. 87, pg. 119
Tea cosy, 20th century
Unmarked, h 42 cm,
VM 92.63.31

cat. 88, pg. 120
Neapolitan Christmas crib doll:
Black King, Italy,
mid 18th century
Unmarked: accredited to the
Bernini school, h 35 cm,
VM 55.2.22

cat. 89, pg. 121
Doll, late 19th – early
20th century.
Unmarked, h 7 cm,
VM 92.63.58

cat. 90, pg. 122
Girls doll, late 19th century
Unmarked, h 37 cm,
VM 58.53.7

cat. 91, pg. 123
Girls doll, late 19th-early
20th century
Unmarked, h 44 cm,
VM 54.38.1

cat. 92, pg. 124
Girls doll, France (?),
1870-1890
Unmarked: J.Steiner (?),
h 45 cm, VM 60.88.12.

cat. 93, pg. 125
Baby doll: 'Roozeke',
2nd half 19th century
Unmarked, h 27 cm,
VM 60.9.168

cat. 94, pg. 126
Boys doll, early 20th century
Unmarked, h 10.5 cm,
VM 87.25.6

cat. 95, pg. 126
Girls doll, early 20th century
Unmarked, h 10.5 cm,
VM 87.25.8

cat. 96, pg. 127
Baby doll, early 20th century
Marked: 701 (on back),
h 11 cm, VM 92.63.33

cat. 97, pg. 127
Girls doll, 19th – 20th century
Unmarked, h 22 cm,
VM 54.38.2.

cat. 98, pg. 128
Girls doll, 19th-20th century
Unmarked, h 14 cm,
VM 59.14.820

cat. 99, pg. 129
Clown, late 19th-early
20th century
Unmarked, h 49 cm,
VM 59.14.818

cat. 100, pg. 130
Rag doll, USA,
early 20th century
Marked: Art Fabric Mills/
Patented/ Feb. 13-1900,
h 58 cm, VM 89.75.11

cat. 101, pg. 131
Doll, 19th century
Unmarked, h 62 cm,
VM 92.63.5

cat. 102, pg. 132
Girls doll, Belgium,
circa 1970
Marked: Unica Belgium,
h 48 cm, VM 88.52.1

cat. 103, pg. 133
Swaddling clothed doll, Belgium,
19th century
Unmarked, h 20 cm,
VM 4642

cat. 104, pg. 133
Swaddling clothed doll, Belgium,
19th century
Unmarked, h 16.5 cm,
VM 4643

cat. 105, pg. 134
Doll, 19th – 20th century
Unmarked, h 29 cm,
VM 4841

cat. 106, pg. 133
Doll, 20th century
Unmarked, h 42 cm,
VM 4646

cat. 107, pg. 135
Doll, 20th century
Unmarked, h 37cm,
VM 4651

cat. 108, pg. 136
Doll, 20th century
Unmarked, h 56 cm,
VM 92.63.39

cat. 109, pg. 136
Doll, 20th century
Unmarked, h 15 cm,
VM 92.63.40

cat. 110, pg. 22
Rag doll, early 20th century
Unmarked, h 42 cm,
VM 4657

cat. 111, pg. 137
Doll: tennis player, 20th century.
Unmarked, h 16 cm,
VM 9820

cat. 112, pg. 137
Dolls: dancing pair, 20th century
Unmarked, h 7 cm, VM 9824

cat. 113, pg. 138
Dolls heads, 19th century
Unmarked, h 7 cm,
VM 4430-4431, 5283-5292,
5294-5296, 5445-5418

cat. 114, pg. 24
Peg wooden doll, Germany,
20th century
Unmarked: Grödnertal,
h 32 cm, VM 5325

cat. 115, pg. 139
Peg wooden doll, Germany:
Grödnertal, 19th century
Unmarked, h 41 cm,
VM 92.63.29

cat. 116, pg. 140
Peg wooden doll, Germany:
Grödnertal, mid 19th century
Unmarked, h 32 cm,
VM 4654

cat. 117, pg. 141
Poupard, (chubby baby doll)
France (?), 19th century
Unmarked, h 27 cm,
VM 92.63.21

cat. 118, pg. 142
Poupard, (chubby baby doll)
France (?), 19th century
Unmarked, h 18 cm,
VM 59.14.714

cat. 119, pg. 143
Poupard, (chubby baby doll)
France (?), 19th century
Unmarked, h 24 cm,
VM 5901

cat. 120, pg. 144
Dolls head, Germany,
early 20th century
Marked: SH 1079 -4 Dep
Germany (= Simon and Halbig), h 8 cm, VM 92.63.16

cat. 121, pg. 28
Dolls head, Germany,
early 20th century
Marked: 370 AM 12/0
Armand Marseille Made in
Germany, h 11 cm,
VM 92.63.17

cat. 122, pg. 145
Dolls head: babies head,
Germany, early 20th century
Marked: AM Armand Marseille, h 11 cm, VM 92.63.20

cat. 123, pg. 145
Dolls head, mid 19th century
Marked: 26, h 7 cm,
VM 5460

cat. 124, pg. 146
Doll, late 19th-early
20th century
Marked: Dep 4, h 73 cm,
VM 92.63.24

cat. 125, pg. 147
Mould, Belgium, 20th century
Marked: Unica Belgium,
h 13.5 cm, VM 73.12.2

cat. 126, pg. 148
Doll, Belgium, 20th century
Marked: Made in Belgium,
h 49 cm, VM 92.63.9

cat. 127, pg. 26
Girls doll: pumpkin head,
19th century
Unmarked, h 70 cm,
VM 92.63.3

cat. 128, pg. 27
Doll, early 20th century
Unmarked, h 72 cm,
VM 60.132.1

Bibliography

- *Album als herinnering aan den prijskamp en tentoonstelling,* Antwerp, 1916.
- *Altes Spielzeug. Sammlung H.G. Klein. Niederrheinisches Freilichtmuseum Grefrath,* Cologne, 1979.
- BACHMANN, M. en HANSMANN, C., *Das grosse Puppenbuch,* Leipzig, 1988.
- BAYER, L., *Das Spielzeugmuseum der Stadt Nürnberg,* Nurenburg, 1978.
- BRECHT, U., *Kostbare Puppen,* Weingarten, 1980.
- BURKIJ – BARTELINK, *Antiek speelgoed,* Bussum, 1975.
- CHARRIER, R., *Franse poppen en mode,* Wissel, s.a.
- CHATEAU, J., *L'enfant et le jeu,* Paris, 1950.
- CIESLIK, J. en M., *Das grosse Schildkröt-Buch. Celluloid Puppen von 1896-1956,* Koslar, 1986.
- CIESLIK, J. en M., *Puppen. Europäische Puppen 1806 bis 1930,* Munich, 1979.
- CLARETIE, L., *Une exposition de poupées à Liège,* in *Lectures modernes,* jg. 2, Brussels, 1903.
- CLARETIE, L., *Les jouets. Histoire-fabrication,* Paris, s.a.
- COLEMAN, D., E. en E., *The collector's encyclopedia of dolls,* Vol. 1, London, 1968.
- COLEMAN, D., E. en E., *The collector's encyclopedia of dolls,* Vol. 2, London, 1986.
- COLLIER, J., *The official identification and price guide to Antique and modern dolls,* New York, 1989.
- d'ALLEMAGNE, H.R., *Histoire des jouets,* Paris, 1903.
- EATON, F., *Poppen in kleur,* Baarn, 1976.
- *Exposition des poupées folkloriques. Miniatures de la collection signées Lilette,* (exhibition-cat.), Fosses-la-Ville, 1968.
- FOURNIER, E., *Histoire des jouets et des jeux d'enfants,* Paris, 1889.
- FRASER, A., *Puppen,* Frankfurt(Main),1963.
- FRASER, A., *Spielzeug. Die Geschichte der Spielzeugs in aller Welt,* Oldenburg, 1966.
- GERWAT-CLARK, B., *The collector's book of dolls,* London, 1987.
- GOODFELLOW, C., *Het eindeloze poppenboek,* De Bilt, 1993.
- HERMAN, P., *Le jouet en Belgique,* Brussels, 1984.
- HERMAN, P., *Poppen made in Belgium,* Brussels, 1988.
- HIRN, Y., *Les jeux d'enfants,* Paris, 1926.
- *Huis Dugasse: Internationale poppententoonstelling,* Antwerp, 1934.
- *Internationale tentoonstelling van oude en moderne poppen,* Antwerp, 1934
- *Internationale tentoonstelling van oude en moderne poppen. Officieel programma,* Antwerp, 1934.
- *Les jouets,* in *Jardin des Arts,* nr. 74, Paris, 1960-61.
- *Jouets. Une sélection du Musée Sonneberg R.D.A.,* (exhibitioncat.), Paris, 1973-'74.
- *Kinderspielzeug. Sonderausstellung Schweizerisches Museum für Volkskunde,* Basel, 1964-'65.
- *Kinderwelt – Museum Schloss Walchen,* Salzkammergut, s.a.
- KING, C.E., *The collector's history of dolls,* London, 1977.
- KRAFT, B. (ed.), *Traumwelt der Puppen,* (exhibitioncat.), Munich, 1991-'92.
- MATHES, R., *Dolls, toys and childhood,* Cumberland Maryland, 1987.
- *Poppenhuizen,* (Rijksmuseum. Facetten der verzameling, nr. 2), Amsterdam, 1955.
- NICOLLE, H., *Les jouets, ce qu'il y a dedans,* Paris, 1869.
- POST, J.W.P., *Het Nederlandsch kinderspel vóór de zeventiende eeuw,* Den Haag, 1914.
- RETTER, H., *Spielzeug. Handbuch zur Geschichte und Pädagogik der Spielmittel,* Weinheim – Basel, 1979.
- RICHTER, L., *Das grosse Buch der schönsten Puppen,* Munich, 1991.
- RICHTER, L., *Die schönsten deutschen Puppen,* Augsburg, 1993.
- RICHTER, L. en J., *Puppen Raritäten,* Munich, 1990.
- SEYFFERT, O. en TRIER, W., *Spielzeug,* Berlin, s.a.
- SEZAN, C., *Les poupées anciennes,* Paris, 1930.
- *A showing of paper-dolls and other cut-out toys from the collection of Wilbur Macey Stone,* Newark, 1931-'32.
- *Sotheby's. Important mechanical musical instruments and automata, fine apprentice and miniature furniture, toys and dolls,* London, june 1994.
- *Sotheby's. Fine dolls, doll's houses, teddy bears, automata,* London, may 1990.
- *Spel en speelgoed door de eeuwen heen,* Mechelen, 1980.
- *Spielzeug aus den Sammlungen der Staatlichen Museen zu Berlin.* (exhibitioncat.), Berlin, 1976.
- *Spielwelten der Kinder an Rhein und Maas,* Cologne, 1993.
- STAP-LOOS, A., *Speelgoed van alle tijden,* Koog aan de Zaan, 1980.
- TOSA, M., *Poupées,* in *Antiquités et Objets d'Art,* nr. 3, Paris, 1990.
- *Van spel, poppen en poppenspel,* (exhibitioncat.), Kontich, november 1975.
- VON BOEHN, M., *Dolls,* New York, 1972.
- WHITE, G., *Toys, dolls, automata. Marks and labels,* London, 1985.
- WITTKOP-MENARDEAU, G., *Von Puppen und Marionetten. Kleine Kulturgeschichte für Sammler und Liebhaber,* Zurich, s.a.

Colophon

This publication appears in conjunction with the exhibition *The dream world of dolls From the collection of the Museum of Folklore, Antwerp* In the Museum of Folklore, Gildekamersstraat 2-6, 2000 Antwerp From 17 December 1994 to 31 March 1995

COORDINATION

Dr. Francine de Nave, Director of the Historical Museums, Frank Herreman, Assistant Director of the Museums of Ethnography and Folklore, Mireille Holsbeke, Scientific assistant, of the Museums of Ethnography and Folklore.

EXHIBITION

Scientific preparation and research:
Patricia Vansummeren.
Restoration and conservation:
Françoise Therry, Ursula Van de Bult, Ann Op de Beeck.
Concept:
Ann Op de Beeck, Mireille Holsbeke, Patricia Vansummeren.
Technical work:
Mick Blancquaert, Barbara Boey, Gustaaf Saenen and the Department of Works.
Collaborators:
the administrative and security staff of the Museum of Folklore.

CATALOGUE

Contributors:
Katharina Engels (Dutch reworking M. Wellens), Mireille Holsbeke, Françoise Therry, Patricia Vansummeren.
Catalogue descriptions:
Patricia Vansummeren.
Editors:
Frank Herreman and Mireille Holsbeke.
Translation:
Karen Shutte.
Photography:
Bart Huysmans, City of Antwerp cultural department.
Photographical documents:
Guy Hutsebaut.
Concept and design:
Griet Van Haute.
Printer:
Snoeck-Ducaju & Zoon
Publishers:
Snoeck-Ducaju & Zoon and the City of Antwerp.
Copyright:
The authors.

D/1994/0012/43
ISBN 90-5349-155-4